STEAM KIDS
IN THE KITCHEN

science / technology / engineering / art / math
activities and recipes for kids

by:
Anne Carey
Amber Scardino
Ana Dziengel
Andra Weber
Chelsey Marashian
Dayna Abraham
Erica Clark
Jamie Hand
Karyn Tripp
Leslie Manlapig
P.R. Newton

First Edition | 2018

ISBN-13: 978-1986069649
ISBN-10: 1986069648

http://steamkidsbooks.com

Cover design by Anne Carey
Book design by Ana Dziengel and Anne Carey
Photography by all authors

Safety Note: Adult supervision required for all activities in this book. Appropriate and reasonable caution is required at all times. The authors of this book disclaim all liability for any damage, mishap or injury that may occur while engaging in activities featured in this book.

Find something you're passionate about and keep tremendously interested in it.

- Julia Child

**We dedicate this book to our children
because they inspire us
to try, to learn, and to teach
something new every day of our lives.**

Table of Contents

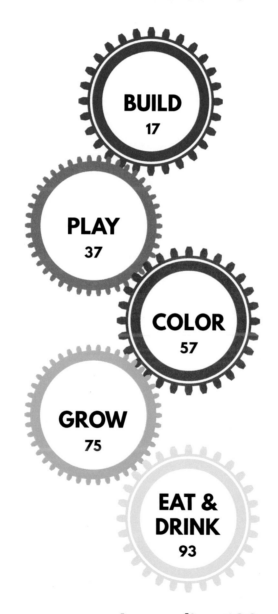

BUILD
17

PLAY
37

COLOR
57

GROW
75

EAT & DRINK
93

BUILD
17

PLAY
37

COLOR
57

GROW
75

**EAT &
DRINK
93**

Introduction

STEAM - Science, Technology, Engineering, Art & Math

STEAM Kids is all about inspiring our next generation of
inventors, innovators and leaders to
question like a scientist | design like a technologist | build like an engineer
create like an artist | deduce like a mathematician
- and -
play like a kid.

And now... cook like a chef too!!

Break out the spatulas, open the fridge, and unlock your creativity!
Inside this book you'll find 70+ activities and recipes you and the kids are going to love.
Bonus sections will help kids learn about the amazing science behind the food they eat, the innovators who
have changed our world through the kitchen, and fun stuff like kitchen careers and more.

We're a group of engineers, teachers,
math nerds, art lovers and writers who all believe that
STEAM is important for children to experience and learn.
And that STEAM can be absolutely, totally, FUN!
We hope you have a blast playing and learning in the kitchen!

What's the STEAM Behind It?

This wouldn't be a STEAM book without helping kids learn a little bit about the meaning and lessons
behind the projects. Look for the "What's the STEAM Behind It?" section to learn things like
the science of density, what's inside the Earth, and what happens when bread rises.
Also look for the STEAM bubbles to see which category the project falls in.
They're perfect for when a child shows interest in a particular subject.

Difficulty

This book is intended for ages 4 to 10, but some activities can be adapted for younger and older children
with a few changes. The projects are rated for difficulty on a scale of 1 to 5 based on the average capabilities
of a 7 year old. Look for the dots on each activity, which will tell you what to expect. Each project also offers
ways to add different challenges for children. The appendix includes a full list of extension activities.

● ● ● ● ●

Safety Note

The projects in this book are intended to be performed under adult supervision. Appropriate and reasonable
caution is recommended when activities call for any items that could be of risk, including, but not limited
to: sharp tools, hot items, chemicals, batteries, scissors and small items that could present a choking hazard.
Please reference the full Kitchen Safety section for more details.
If you are unsure of the safety or age appropriateness of an activity, please consult your child's doctor.

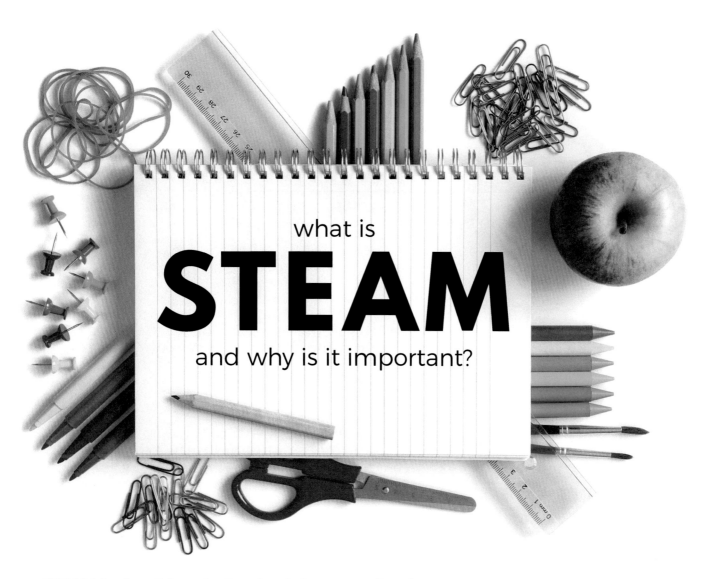

what is
STEAM
and why is it important?

STEAM is the abbreviation for Science, Technology, Engineering, Art & Math.
It's an integrated approach to learning that encourages students
to think more broadly about real-world problems.

STEAM helps kids:

- **Ask questions**
- **Connect the dots**
- **Problem solve**
- **Think creatively**
- **Be innovative**

Why do we need the A in STEAM?

Because art makes STEM better! Here are some of the concrete benefits of incorporating the arts into science:

- It helps remove idea inhibition (there's no wrong answer in art!).
- It focuses on the process which helps drive innovation.
- It teaches the power of observation, of people and your surroundings.
- It helps hone spatial awareness and mathematical concepts like geometry.

KITCHEN SAFETY

Tips for managing hot stuff, sharp tools, and other kitchen rules that help keep kids safe.

Before you begin any of the experiments in the STEAM Kids Kitchen book, please take the time to review proper kitchen safety protocol with your children. The STEAM Kids team recommends that children who perform any or all of the experiments in this book do so with appropriate adult supervision.

Kids are curious! The purpose behind all of our STEAM Kids books is to foster the innate curiosity of our children. But of course, we want to make sure that the same curiosity we love so much does not lead to accidents or injury. While the kitchen does harbor potential dangers, with proper instruction, children can learn how to use almost any kitchen implement and tool safely.

The following is not meant to be an exhaustive list of kitchen safety tips. The STEAM Kids team encourages you to research more about kitchen safety and to install childproofing latches and protections as appropriate for your family.

Remember, the STEAM Kids team wants you to remain safe while learning, exploring and playing. You are responsible for the safety and well-being of your children. If you are ever concerned about your child's safety immediately stop any kitchen experiment or project.

keep it clean

Kitchen hygiene is important!!
- Wash hands. Teach your children to always to wash their hands before and after touching food, especially after handling raw food like meat or eggs. This is also good advice to follow before conducting science experiments. You don't want bacteria or dirt from your hands corrupting your scientific data!
- Clear the area of unnecessary items before beginning a project. Keeping the area clear of clutter will help reduce the chance of accidents or injuries. It will also help keep everyone's attention on the project.
- Be sure to clean surfaces with disinfectant after handling raw food.
- If you clean along the way, after project clean-up isn't so overwhelming!

Important Safety Gear

Hand and dish soap
Hot pads and oven mitts
Tongs
Safety glasses
Safe place to store sharp tools
Outlet covers
Oven locks

that's hot!

Burns are no fun AND are totally avoidable!
- Educate your children on how to safely operate appliances and always supervise.
- Instruct children to steer clear of hot stoves and ovens. Use your best judgement as to whether or not your children are responsible enough to operate the equipment themselves. Using the back burners is safer than using front burners. Certain substances, such as oil or sugar will burn skin very easily when hot, and should be handled only by adults.
- Keep hands and flammable items away from the stove and oven. Keep items such as oven mitts, dishrags and paper towels away from heat.
- Use oven mitts to protect hands when handling hot items.
- Teach children about fire safety. A responsible adult should learn how to operate, and keep a fire extinguisher in or near the kitchen. You can also use baking soda, or a large pot lid to smother small fires.

be tool smart

The right tools used the right way make it easier!
- Educate your children on how to safely operate appliances and always supervise.
- Do not plug in appliances with wet hands.
- Use safety plugs to cover any unused electrical outlets and try to do any project that uses liquid away from outlets.
- If using boxed rolls of plastic wrap, aluminum foil or similar materials, ensure children know how to keep their fingers away from the serrated edge.
- If experiments use materials that fizz or splash, wear protective eye wear.
- Keep hands away from moving parts, such as mixing blades.
- Keep knives out of reach of small hands. Instruct children on the proper use of knives and other sharp tools.
- Be aware of what appliances are on and hot. And be sure to turn off, and unplug appliances after use. Do not allow cords to dangle or get wrapped around items.
- Don't put metal items in the microwave.

can i eat that?

Not all kitchen projects are edible!
- Keep all poisons and toxic materials, such as rubbing alcohol out of reach of children. Place in high cupboards or behind a locked door.
- Even though experiments in this book use food, unless the project specifically says otherwise, do not eat or taste any of the projects, or any of the materials.
- Consuming raw or undercooked meats, poultry, seafood, shellfish, eggs or unpasteurized milk may increase your risk of foodborne illness.

FOOD Q&A

These are the hot kitchen topics people are talking about.

What are GMO foods?

GMO stands for a genetically modified organism. GMO's are a unique species that has been created in a laboratory by selecting one gene from a species and inserting it into a different species, creating a new combination of species that does not occur naturally in nature. Usually, this is done to give a species a distinct characteristic like improved shelf life or different color or shape. Corn, soy, canola and sugar beet are the most common GMO food ingredients found in today's food. There is an on-going debate on the effects of GMO produced food. The long-term effects are unknown at this time, but GMO's are allowed in today's conventional farming.

What is Molecular Gastronomy?

Molecular gastronomy is used to describe the physical and chemical transformations that food undergoes while being prepared. This research often broke from away from traditional food innovation such as manufacturing and safety and instead focused as much on the diner's experience as the taste of the food.

Some unusual food processes used in modern cuisine are spherification (turning into a sphere), gelification (turning into gels), and emulsification (dispersing droplets of one liquid into another liquid). These processes combine food and science and create art on your plate!

What does Farm to Table mean?

Farm to Table (or Farm to Fork) is the phrase used to describe the processes that food undergoes from agricultural production to being eaten. These steps may include the farm, food manufacturing, a grocery store, and more.

Currently, there is a social movement that aims to reduce the number of steps in this journey from farm to table and to educate eaters on where our food has been. The Farm to Table movement believes that it is better for food safety and freshness, as well as the environment and economy, to be closer to the farmer in the food chain. An entire culinary community is built upon this movement.

These famous innovators conducted research that changed how we live and eat today.

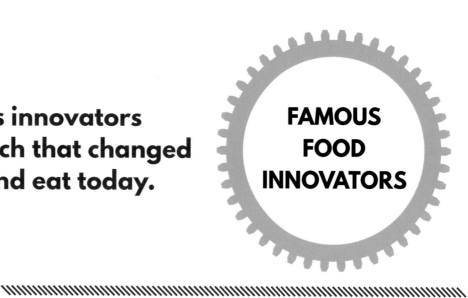

FAMOUS FOOD INNOVATORS

W.K. Kellogg - Father of Breakfast Cereal

W.K. Kellogg is the inventor of Kellogg's Corn Flakes. In the late 1890's, Kellogg worked for his brother, a doctor who ran a sanitarium in Battle Creek, Michigan. It was here that he conducted reasearch on nutrition and healthy diets.

One day when boiling wheat as an easily digestible food, he left the wheat out for several hours. It got soft and Kellogg decided to roll it out like regular bread. The dough separated into flat sections, that when baked became the first corn flakes.

In 1906, he created the Battle Creek Corn Flakes Company, the world's first cereal company.

Louis Pasteur - Inventor of Pasteurization

Louie Pasteur was a French chemist, born in 1822. After earning his doctorate degree at 25 years old, he became a chemistry professor at the University of Strasbourg and later dean at the University of Lille. Throughout his life he made some major contributions to science and improved the lives of millions of people. Not only did he develop vaccinations for diseases such as anthrax, cholera, tuberculosis, and smallpox, he is most well-known for inventing the pasteurization process. Pasteurization involves removing bacteria from wine, beer, and milk by boiling the liquid then cooling it. This process is widely used to this day.

Barbara McClintock - 1st Solo Woman to Win a Nobel Prize

Genes are the building blocks of all living things, yet they are so small they can only be seen with very specialized equipment. One scientist made huge advances in the understanding of genetics. Barbara McClintock was an American scientist and cytogeneticist who was awarded the 1983 Nobel Prize in Physiology or Medicine for her research using maize (i.e. corn). Her award winning theory focused on chromosomes and the impact of 'mobile genetic elements'. These elements influence evolution and genetic mutations. McClintock was a pioneer in the field of genetics and understanding how genetic information was passed down through generations.

RECYLING IN THE KITCHEN

Recycling is important to help protect the natural environment for future generations. Recycling and reusing materials helps prevent pollution, saves energy, creates jobs, and protects wildlife. When it comes to the earth, you are one person alone, but together we are many.

Check your local recycling center to find out what can be recycled in your home town.

Do what you love and you'll never work a day in your life!

Wouldn't it be cool to get paid to be creative, help others, and make things that people enjoy? Becoming a chef does just that! Cooking is an artform that engages all of the senses. A dish has to be visually pleasing, as well as smell and taste good. There is a science to cooking that requires experimentation. A chef uses a plate as a canvas, considers texture, and knows the chemistry behind the ingredients. Inventing a new recipe takes skill and creativity.

But, did you know that becoming a chef isn't the only career that is born in the kitchen!

KITCHEN CAREERS

Love spending time in the kitchen? Here are some cool FOOD CAREERS!

Food stylist
Chef
Kitchen designer
Product developer / R&D chef
Test chef
Restauranteur

Food blogger
Culinary magazine editor
Food photographer
Culinary instructor
Nutritionist
Agricultural scientist

QUESTION LIKE SCIENTISTS with the SCIENTIFIC METHOD

The scientific method is the basic set of actions that scientists use to make new discoveries and prove theories correct or incorrect. Predict, hypothesize, wonder, test, trial and problem solving is where the learning happens. The scientific method is a way to narrate what happens when questions are asked and tested.

The six basic steps of the scientific method are:

1. Make observations.
2. Ask questions.
3. Propose a hypothesis.
4. Design and perform an experiment to test the hypothesis.
5. Analyze the data to see if it supports the hypothesis.
6. Develop a theory based on your results.

If a hypothesis isn't correct, propose and test a new hypothesis based on these findings.

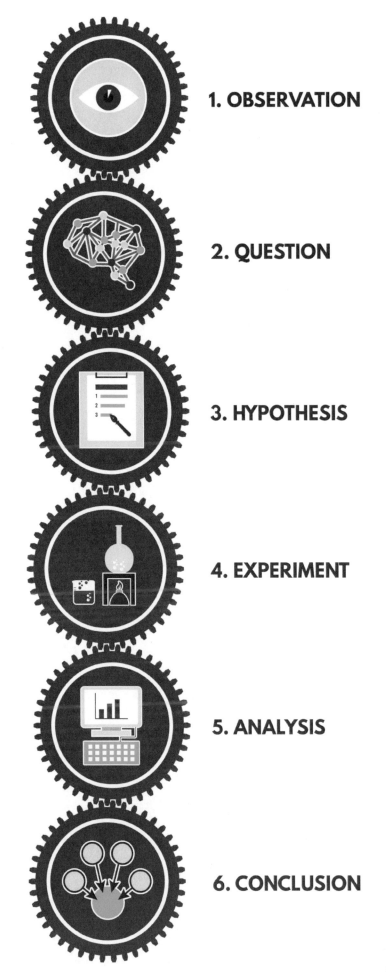

1. OBSERVATION

2. QUESTION

3. HYPOTHESIS

4. EXPERIMENT

5. ANALYSIS

6. CONCLUSION

BUILD

Fruit Circuits

Did you know you can power a light bulb with fruit?

by Anne Carey **Left Brain Craft Brain**

Difficulty: ● ● ● ●

Estimated Project Time: 20 minutes

What's the STEAM behind it?

A **circuit** is a closed path or loop around which an electric current flows. In a fruit circuit, electrons transfer between the zinc nail anode and the copper wire cathode. It takes an electrolyte to make the electricity happen, in this case the citric acid in the lemon and other fruit.

If the circuit is complete, it is called a **closed circuit** and the bulb will get power and light up. If the path is broken, it is an **open circuit** and the bulb will stay dark. There are two types of circuits, Series and Parallel.

In a **series circuit:** Two or more electrical devices are connected end to end in a single path. If the circuit is broken at any spot, none of the devices will work.

In a **parallel circuit:** Two or more electrical devices are connected in a path that splits into two or more branches. If the circuit is open, devices on the broken branch will not work, while other branches will still get power.

Ingredients:
Fruit
(citrus works best, but
experiment with
other kinds, too)
2" Copper nails or wires
2" Zinc nails
Leads with alligator clips
5 or 10 mm LED bulbs
Multi-meter (optional)

  S T E A M

Instructions:

1. Gather your fruit and soften them up to get the juices flowing. This will improve their battery power. You can do this by gently squeezing them in your hands or rolling them on a table.

2. Each piece of fruit in your circuit needs 1 copper nail or wire and 1 zinc nail. Insert them into the fruit as far away from each other as possible, at least 2 inches apart.

3. Connect one alligator clip lead to the zinc nail and one alligator clip lead to the copper nail or wire.

4. Connect the other ends of the alligator clip leads to the LED wires. The lead connected to the zinc nail should attach to the negative lead. The positive LED leads connect to the copper nails. Does it light up?

5. Try adding more fruit and different kinds of fruit. How does the light in the bulb change? Get stronger? Weaker?

6. Add more fruit and LEDs and build a series circuit and a parallel circuit. Can you make all the bulbs light up?

Project Extensions:

- Try using a penny instead of a copper wire. How does this change the LED brightness?

- If you have a multi-meter, use it to measure the voltage in your different fruit circuits. Compare the results.

- For another fun circuit building activity, make this Pop-Up Light-Up Paper Flower Card.

DIY Spring Scale

Build your own spring scale using a plastic cup and slinky to weigh different types of candy.

by Jamie Hand **Kids STEAM Lab**

Ingredients:

Plastic cup
Hole punch
Scissors
String
Slinky
Rubber bands
Table
Ruler
White posterboard
Markers
Variety of candy
Heavy books

Difficulty: ● ● ●

Estimated Project Time: 30 minutes

What's the STEAM behind it?

A spring scale is a type of scale used to measure weight. The slinky is a spring that if you stretch and then let go, it will return to its original shape. The more weight you add the more the slinky stretches. The weight is directly correlated to the length of a spring and can be measured.

S T E A M

Instructions:

1. Start building your spring scale by punching two holes across from each other at the top of your plastic cup.

2. Use string to attach the plastic cup to one end of the slinky.

3. On the opposite end of the slinky, wrap a rubber band around half of the slinky so it stays together.

4. Place a ruler on the edge of a table so that part of the ruler extends out from the table. Place heavy books on the ruler to hold it in place.

5. Slide the closed rubberband part of the slinky over the ruler that extends from the table creating your spring scale.

6. Prop a white poster board behind your spring scale. Mark on the posterboard where the height of the cup is with no candy inside the cup.

7. Place your first candy in the cup. Mark the height of the cup on the posterboard.

8. Take out the first candy and put in a different kind. Mark the height of the cup.

9. Investigate:

   a. Does the second piece of the candy weigh more or less than the first piece?

   b. How does the slinky stretch as you add candy or different weight?

   c. Experiment with different types of candy. Which candy weighed the most? Which weighed the least?

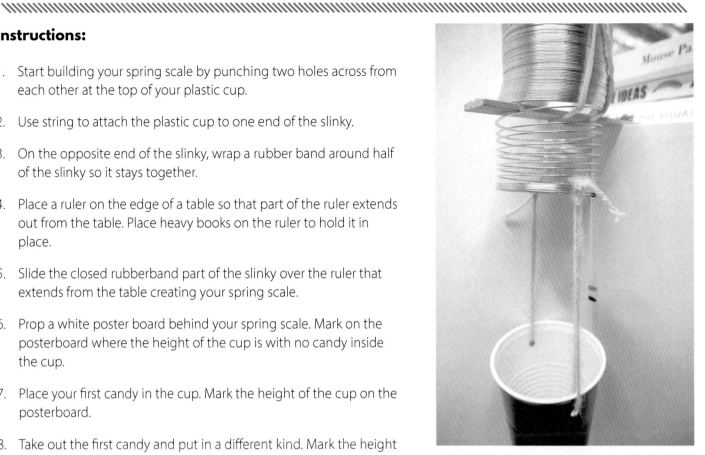

Project Extensions:

- Try calibrating your spring scale with water. Place 25 ml of water in the cup and mark on your poster board. Place 50 ml of water in the cup and mark. Can you use the calibrated markings to make an accurate spring scale to measure weight?

- For another fun engineering project, try this Backyard Pulley.

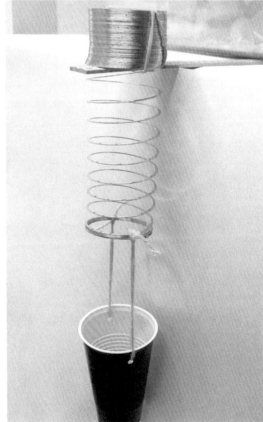

   S T E A M

Ice Building Challenge

How tall can you make your tower before it melts away?

by Dayna Abraham **Lemon Lime Adventures**

Difficulty:

Estimated Project Time: 20 minutes plus several hours freezing time

What's the STEAM behind it?

Building challenges encourage children to discover basic physics principles and test their engineering thinking through design, problem solving, creativity and collaboration.

Salt acts as a magic glue in this challenge. Salt lowers the freezing point of water, creating a liquid layer between cubes. As the temperature continues to decrease, that thin layer of liquid freezes, fusing the cubes together.

Ingredients:
Water
Food coloring (optional)
Silicone muffin cups or ice cube trays
A large tray
Salt

Instructions:

1. The night before doing the ice building challenge, freeze at least 20 ice cubes per child. For colored cubes, add food coloring to the water before freezing.

2. Set out the ice cubes and trays for building.

3. Introduce the bowl of salt as a "glue" to build their towers and castles higher. Challenge the children to build the tallest ice castle.

Project Extensions:

- Add some math to your building session! Count the cubes you used to create your tower or measure your tower with a ruler or measuring tape.

- Draw the castle you designed with your ice cubes. What happens when you change the size of the ice? Can you change the way you stacked the ice?

- Also try this Hands-Free Ice Cube Boat Race.

S T E A M

Toast Stamps

Use aluminum foil, chopsticks, and heat to create art on bread!

by Leslie Manlapig **Pink Stripey Socks**

Difficulty: ●●

Estimated Project Time: 10-15 minutes

What's the STEAM behind it?

Placing bread under the broiler transforms it. The heat removes moisture from the bread, making it harder than before. The portions of bread that are most exposed to the heat also turn brown. This is due to the Maillard reaction occurring between the sugars and amino acids in the bread. This causes the bread to turn brown and tasty!

Instructions:

SAFETY NOTE: Adult supervision required as the oven and stamps are hot.

1. Decorate your bread. There are three ways you can make designs on toasted bread.:

   a. Cut out shapes from a sheet of aluminum foil and place them onto your bread.

   b. Cut out a sheet of aluminum foil, roll it, curve the rolled foil into a certain shape, and place it onto your bread.

   c. Use a chopstick to press down a design on your bread.

2. Place the bread slices onto a baking pan and place under the broiler for a couple of minutes. Make sure to watch the bread so that it doesn't burn! Pull out your toasted bread and remove all aluminum foil shapes to reveal your design.

Ingredients:

**Aluminum foil
Bread
Scissors
Baking pan
Oven
Oven mitt
Chopstick**

Project Extensions:

- Try doing this activity with other baked goods like tortillas or bagels.

- Love learning from food? Try this Maple Syrup Candy!

S T E A M

Electric Dough Robot

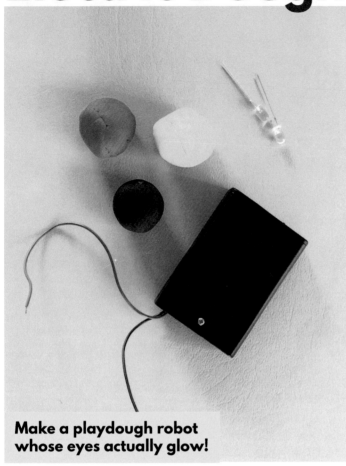

Make a playdough robot whose eyes actually glow!

by Anne Carey **Left Brain Craft Brain**

Difficulty: ● ● ● ● ●

Estimated Project Time: 20 minutes

What's the STEAM behind it?

This project uses Play-Doh and modeling clay to create an electrical circuit that lights up the eyes of STEAM Kids in the Kitchen robot, Toque. The Play-Doh acts as a conductor, a material that can transmit electricity. The modeling clay acts as an insulator, which prevents electricity from flowing.

In order for the robot to glow, there must be a continuous path between a battery pack and an LED with Play-Doh. This is called a closed circuit. If your path breaks, it's called an open circuit.

Ingredients:

Play-Doh
Modeling clay
2 - 10mm diffused LED bulbs
4 AA batteries
4 AA battery pack
with leads (wires)

S T E A M

SAFETY NOTE: Adult supervision and safety glasses are recommended when experimenting with electricity. Never touch battery pack wires to each other or LEDs straight to the battery pack wires as this can cause the components to overheat or be damaged.

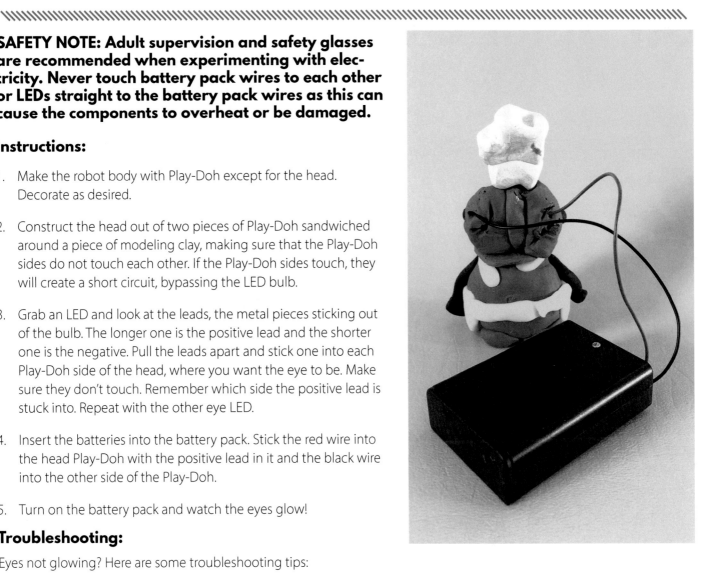

Instructions:

1. Make the robot body with Play-Doh except for the head. Decorate as desired.

2. Construct the head out of two pieces of Play-Doh sandwiched around a piece of modeling clay, making sure that the Play-Doh sides do not touch each other. If the Play-Doh sides touch, they will create a short circuit, bypassing the LED bulb.

3. Grab an LED and look at the leads, the metal pieces sticking out of the bulb. The longer one is the positive lead and the shorter one is the negative. Pull the leads apart and stick one into each Play-Doh side of the head, where you want the eye to be. Make sure they don't touch. Remember which side the positive lead is stuck into. Repeat with the other eye LED.

4. Insert the batteries into the battery pack. Stick the red wire into the head Play-Doh with the positive lead in it and the black wire into the other side of the Play-Doh.

5. Turn on the battery pack and watch the eyes glow!

Troubleshooting:

Eyes not glowing? Here are some troubleshooting tips:

- Try turning the LED around and inserting the long lead into the other half of the head. You may have had them backwards.

- Check that each side of the Play-Doh head is completely insulated from the other with modeling clay, i.e. they don't touch.

- Are your batteries and bulbs fresh? Try new ones if they aren't working.

Project Extensions:

 Design a robot with more lights than just the eyes. What do you have to do to make it work? Add another battery pack? Does it need more modeling clay insulator?

 For another fun robot project, try this Robot Playdough with Deconstructed Computer Parts.

DIY Solar Oven

Who needs a fire pit for s'mores when you've got science?

by Dayna Abraham **Lemon Lime Adventures**

Difficulty: ● ● ●

Estimated Project Time: 45 minutes

What's the STEAM behind it?

The solar oven works because it converts sunlight into heat energy. This energy can then be used for cooking. It works best when the box is covered in a reflective material that catches as much sunlight as possible. The tin foil used in this cooker ensures that the majority of sunlight is caught and used.

Black retains heat and light, making it the perfect cooking surface in your oven. As heat is held by the construction paper, the air molecules in the oven are heated as well. The rise in the air temperature transfers heat to the s'mores, melting the delicious chocolate and marshmallows.

Ingredients:

Pizza box
2 Clear sheet protectors
Black construction paper
Tape (clear & duct)
Utility blade
Thermometer
Bamboo skewer
Glue
Tin foil
Ruler
Pen

Marshmallows
Chocolate
Graham crackers

S T E A M

Instructions:

SAFETY NOTE: Adult supervision required as the oven will get hot.

1. Be sure to do this activity on a hot sunny day for best results.

2. Make a window on the top of the box by measuring a square two inches from the sides and cutting three sides with the straight edge.

3. Line the box and lid with tin foil and secure black construction paper to the bottom with tape.

4. Separate the plastic sheet protectors into single layers and use the plastic to cover the opening on top of the pizza box. Tape the sides so that the plastic is as tight as you can get it.

5. Now prop up the foil covered flap in the lid by attaching skewers to the side of the box with tape. T

6. Place graham cracker, chocolate, marshmallow stacks on the black paper and place your thermometer in the box. Close lid with plastic, making sure the foil covered lid is propped up. Set a timer and see just how long it takes to make your s'mores.

Project Extensions:

- Think about some design changes you could make to the oven. What happens if you leave the foil off the lid? Does it take more or less time to cook the s'mores? What happens if you move your oven to the shade? What else can you cook?

- For another kitchen science experiment, check out this <u>Sinking Soda Surprise</u> activity.

S T E A M

Kitchen Mini Makerspace

Use recycled materials to create a Mini Maker Space.

by Leslie Manlapig **Pink Stripey Socks**

Difficulty: ●
Estimated Project Time: 20 minutes

Kitchen Supplies

**Plastic containers
(cleaned and dried)
Cardboard (paper towel rolls,
cereal boxes, etc.)
Rubber bands
Tin cans
Bottle caps
Disposable plates, cups, utensils
Kitchen tools
(egg beaters, strainers, etc.)
Corks
Aluminum foil**

Craft Supplies

**Pencils and markers
Scissors
Glue (hot glue gun
and white or tacky glue)
Tape (clear and masking)
String
Hole punchers
Stickers
Paper
Paper clips**

What's the STEAM behind it?

When given free reign to choose materials and projects, children take initiative in imagining, designing, and experimenting. They can explore the properties of materials and problem solve in a way that is meaningful to them. These practices are crucial for STEAM learning.

S T E A M

Instructions:

1. Put out a variety of kitchen items, recycled items, and crafting items.

2. Encourage children to explore, design, and build! They can build something according to their own imagination. Or, you can give them open-ended building prompts like the ones below:

   a. Build the tallest / longest / strongest, etc.

   b. Do seasonal challenges like trap the Easter bunny or a Leprechaun, design a sled for Santa.

   c. Design a dream space or piece of architecture like a kitchen, zoo, bedroom, school, amusement park, bridge, space station, etc.

   d. Build a vehicle or tool that rolls, moves something, flies, shoots, floats, or drives.

Project Extensions:

- Ask children questions like, "Can you tell me what you're working on? Did this work the way you wanted it to? How would you build this differently? What other materials could you have used instead?"

- For more recycled tinkering projects, try this DIY Conveyor Belt or Tin Can Toy Car.

Straw Quills

Make "quill" pens from straws with this easy and creative tutorial.

by Leslie Manlapig **Pink Stripey Socks**

Difficulty:

Estimated Project Time: 10 minutes

What's the STEAM behind it?

People used quills before pens were invented. They were created by cutting the tips of bird feathers a certain way. The hollow center stem of a feather, the shaft, is especially good for holding ink. Here, we're cutting our straw to mimic a quill pen.

Ingredients:
Scissors
Straws (varying sizes)
Food coloring (or liquid watercolors)
Palette or cups to hold the watercolors
Paper

Instructions:

1. Cut the tip of the straws at an angle to mimic quill pens.

2. Dip the cut end into food coloring to use your "quill" pen. Create!

3. Explore different quills:

   a. Try making pens from different sized straws (e.g. stirrers or bubble tea straws). Compare the results. Which ones work best?

   b. Try cutting the tips of the straws at different angles. How do the different angles affect how the pens write?

Project Extensions:

- Find a feather and try cutting the tip to create a quill pen. Now compare your feather pens and straw pens. Which works better?

- Try this Spinning Top Marker Art for another DIY art supply activity.

  T E

DIY Thermometer

Measure hot and cold with this simple kitchen thermometer.

by Dayna Abraham **Lemon Lime Adventures**

Difficulty: ● ● ●

Estimated Project Time: 20 minutes

What's the STEAM behind it?

Water is comprised of molecules that when heated create bonds and expand. By creating a sealed environment for the water, when the water is heated, it has nowhere to expand to except to rise in the thermometer. The same is true when water gets cold. The molecular bonds shrink, making the water level lower.

Ingredients:
Water
Rubbing alcohol
Recycled glass bottle
Clear straw
Measuring cup
Sticky tack
Cooking oil, any kind
Pipette or eye dropper
Red food color, optional

Instructions:

1. Fill half of the bottle with water and the rest with rubbing alcohol, making sure the liquid comes to the top of the bottle.

2. Add a few drops of food coloring to make it easier to see the changes in the water level.

3. Insert a straw in the lid and surround the straw with sticky tack to create a good seal.

4. With a pipette, add a few drops of the colored liquid to the straw until about 2 inches show.

5. Finally, add one drop of cooking oil to the straw. This will create a seal.

6. With a thin-lined permanent marker, mark the line of the liquid as your base-line temperature.

7. To read the thermometer, watch the liquid level rise for warmer temperatures and fall for colder temperatures.

Project Extensions:

● Compare the DIY thermometer with a purchased version over several days. Place both thermometers in location and mark the water level in the bottle at different temperatures with the reading from the purchased thermometer. Also check out this Weather Jar experiment!

 S T E A M

Snack Mix Machine

Make snacktime fun with this simple machine building challenge.

by Anne Carey **Left Brain Craft Brain**

Difficulty: ● ● ● ● ●

Estimated Project Time: 30 minutes

Ingredients:

Snack mix ingredients
(see snack mix blend ideas)
Paper and pencil
Cardboard and other recyclables
(milk cartons, paper towel rolls,
plastic bowls, etc.)
Materials that could be used for
axles like dowel rods or PVC pipe
Rope or twine for pulleys
Screws and screwdriver
Wood or other materials
for wedges
Cups or bowls
Tape and/or glue
Scissors

Snack Mix Blend Ideas

- **Tropical Rainbow:** Rainbow Goldfish crackers || Tropical dried fruit mix || Toasted corn kernels

- **Going Nuts:** Cashews || Peanuts || Popcorn

- **S'mores:** Mini graham crackers || Marshmallows || Chocolate chips

- **Choco-berry:** Pretzels || Dried cranberries || Chocolate chips

- **PB&J:** Pretzels || Peanut butter chips || Dried cranberries

- **Create Your Own:** Pick three of your favorite snacks and mix.

S T E A M

What's the STEAM behind it?

This project is a perfect opportunity to learn about simple machines, the building blocks of all things that move. Here are the six types of simple machines:

Lever: A stiff board that rests on a center turning point called a fulcrum that is used to lift objects. Think teeter totter.

Inclined plane: A hard, flat surface with one end higher than the other. Aids in moving objects. Think slide.

Wheel and axle: A wheel with a rod attached to the middle that can help lift objects. Think bicycle.

Wedge: Two inclined planes put together and helps push objects apart. Think axe.

Pulley: Adds a rope to a wheel which allows you to change direction of a force. Think flagpole or window blinds.

Screw: An inclined plane wrapped around a pole that can lift objects or hold them together. Think screw.

Instructions:

Challenge Rules

This is an open-ended building challenge, but it does have two rules.

1. The machine must be able to mix at least two different kinds of snacks.

2. It must use two different types of simple machines to get the job done.

Design, Build, Test!

Work like an engineer and design your machine on paper first. Think about the supplies, what the end mix goal is, etc. Then build it.

Then test it and snack. Rethink the design if it doesn't quite work the first time. Or change up the flavor mixtures.

The biggest thing to remember here is that this project is about the process, not necessarily the end result. Because that's where the learning happens.

Project Extensions:

- Design some machines that can make cooking easier. What do they do? Is it based upon existing machines like microwaves, stoves, blenders, etc.?

- For another fun engineering project with recyclables, try this Recycled Suspension Bridge.

 S T E A M

Building Challenge Materials

Food

Small fruit pieces (cucumber slices, apple chunks, strawberry pieces, orange slices or peels, grapes. etc.)
Sugar cubes
Cheese cubes
Bread cubes
Potato chunks

Various types of dried pasta
Small candies (gummy bears, jelly beans, gumdrops, taffy)
Marshmallows
Raisins
Dried cranberries
Pretzel sticks

Connectors & Supports

Toothpicks
Straws
Popsicle sticks
Pipe cleaners
String or yarn
Homemade playdough
Foil pieces
Wooden skewers
Cotton swabs

Tools

Paper
Timers
Rulers
Scales
Measuring tape
Camera
Journal
Pencils
Art supplies

Food Building Challenges

Make some delicious creations with these food building challenges.

by Chelsey Marashian **Buggy & Buddy**

Difficulty: ●● **Estimated Project Time:** 30 minutes

What's the STEAM behind it?

By creating various structures, children gain experience exploring physics concepts like gravity, stability, and balance, as well as practice in engineering and design. Building with food lends itself well to art and math integration. As children design, they are creating sculptures and exploring architecture. They can combine various colors of foods to create all kinds of interesting designs and patterns in their creations. Young children can also be encouraged to count the number of items used in each creation.

Instructions:

1. Place an assortment of food (about 2-3 choices) and connectors & supports (1-3 options) on a paper plate. If doing this with multiple children at once, give them different variations and assortments on their own paper plates. Also be sure each child has access to scissors.

2. Have the child brainstorm ways they could use the provided materials to build. Encourage them to try out different ways to use the materials.

3. Invite the child to build a structure using only the materials on his or her plate.

4. Discuss the creation. Use questions/statements like these to promote a discussion: Tell me about what you built. Does it remind you of anything in the real world? What was the most challenging part of building your structure? What was the easiest? How did you come up with your idea? How could you modify it? How many _____ did you use in your structure?

5. Optional: Encourage the child to illustrate his or her creation on paper or in a journal or photograph the build.

Project Extensions:

● Make a set of directions for creating your structure to give to a friend so they can build the same creation. Include a list of materials needed and a detailed set of instructions. See how similar their design looks to yours!

● Try these Mystery Bag Challenges for more open-ended building prompts.

S T E A M

PLAY

Soda & Mentos Geysers

How high will the soda fly in this fun chemical reaction?

by Dayna Abraham **Lemon Lime Adventures**

Ingredients:

Notebook and pencil
2 liter or 20 oz. soda bottles
(multiple kinds for
more test variables)
Mentos
Paper (optional)
Yardstick or measuring tape
(optional)

Difficulty: ● ● ●

Estimated Project Time: 20 minutes

What's the STEAM behind it?

The explosion you see when you mix mentos and soda, is something called "nucleation". In essence, it is the result of tiny bubbles of carbon dioxide clinging to the imperfections and holes in the surface of the mentos. Since the mentos are heavy and sink to the bottom of the bottle, the bubbles push the liquid up and out of the bottle.

S T E A M

Instructions:

1. First plan out the test variables for the experiments and write down the different options in a notebook. Pick one thing to test at a time (size of soda bottle, number of mentos, or type of soda).

2. Line up the soda bottles next to each other according to the planned experiments.

3. Roll a piece of paper into a tube (for easy distribution of mentos) and add the mentos to the paper tube.

4. Carefully, but quickly, release the mentos into the soda and stand back to watch how high the explosion goes.

5. Estimate how high the soda flew and write down in the experiment notebook.

6. Repeat the tests over and over testing different variables until you have found the perfect combination to create maximum fizz.

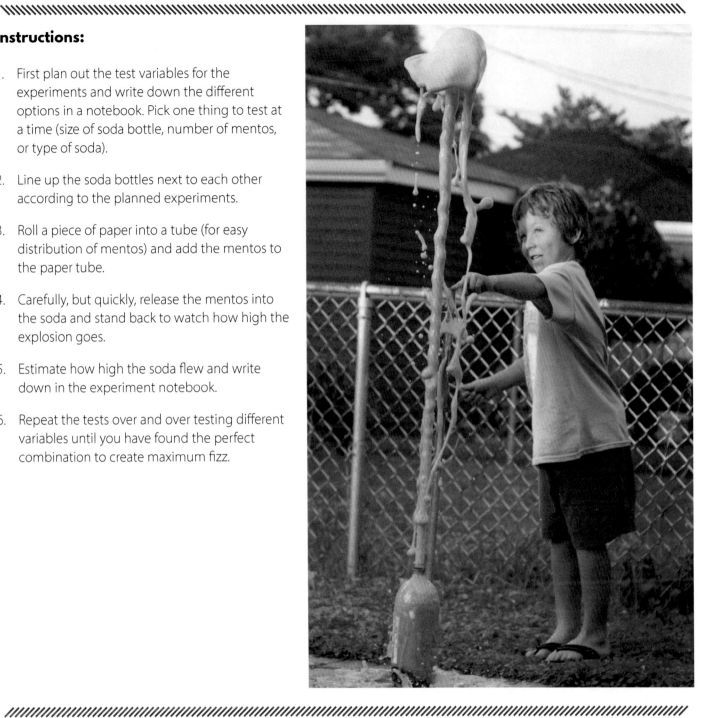

Project Extensions:

- Want to see more examples of nucleation? Drop different materials into a soda and watch what happens. Raisins dance around like they are at a party, while salt creates a fizzing foaming mess. What else could you try?

- Also check out these colorful Rainbow Reactions!

Egg Walking

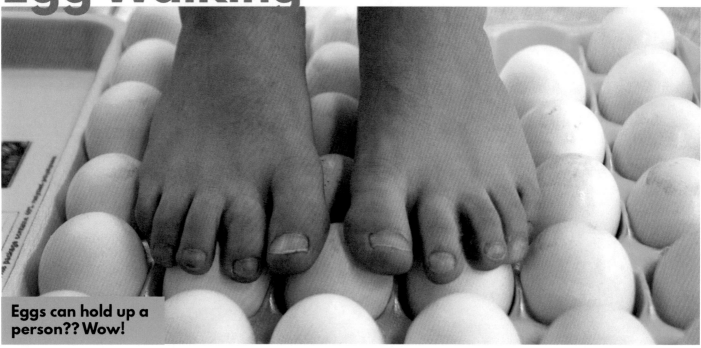

Eggs can hold up a person?? Wow!

by Amber Scardino **Figment Creative Labs**

Difficulty: ● ●

Estimated Project Time: 15 minutes

What's the STEAM behind it?

Walking on eggs seems impossible, but the dome shape of an egg is actually one of the strongest in nature and in architecture. A dome shape distributes weight and pressure across the entire shape so no one point bears the bulk of the load. The trick to not cracking an egg is to apply equal pressure to both ends at the same time.

Ingredients:

Trash bag to protect area
Eggs (4-8 dozen)
Egg cartons
Feet
Soap or disinfectant
to clean area
Towel for clean up, since let's
face it, this takes practice.

Instructions:

1. Put down a trash bag or make sure you are working in an easily cleanable area. Just in case.

2. Don't wear any jewelry that may throw off the experiment.

3. Test the strength of an egg. Hold an egg tight in the palm of your hand hand, wrapping your fingers around it. Apply even pressure.

4. Make sure all the eggs in the carton are facing the same direction.

5. Have someone lower you onto the eggs where your feet and weight are evenly covering the eggs.

6. Have more eggs? Keep walking, with weight evenly distributed.

Project Extensions:

● Try using things other than an egg carton to hold the eggs in place.

● Place something flat on top of the eggs. For example, see how many books the eggs can hold layed flat on top. If you place a flat board on top, can you walk across?

S T E A M

Dinosaur Eggs

Make these surprise eggs hatch with chemistry!

Difficulty: ●●

by P.R. Newton **STEAM Powered Family**

Estimated Project Time: 10 minutes prep, 3 hours freezing time, 10 minutes hatch time

What's the STEAM behind it?

This activity explores the popular baking soda and vinegar reaction. During this chemical reaction, the vinegar reacts with the baking soda. Vinegar or Acetic Acid has the chemical formula CH_3COOH. Baking soda (Sodium Bicarbonate)is a base and has the chemical formula $NaHCO_3$. During this reaction the products are sodium acetate ($NaC_2H_3O_2$), water (H_2O) and carbon dioxide (CO_2). Carbon dioxide is the gas that causes the bubbling during the reaction.

Instructions:

1. Divide the baking soda into separate bowls for each color. One box of baking soda made approximately 3 eggs. Add a few drops of food coloring and mix (wear protective gloves). Add water a teaspoon at a time and mix until it forms a crumbly paste and starts to stick and form.

2. Take a palmful of the paste and squish it about to make a ball. Press in a dinosaur. Then add more paste to the top and sides until the entire dinosaur is encased.

3. Place on parchment paper on a cookie sheet and set in the freezer until frozen.

4. Set the eggs in a large dish and cover the table. This is messy! Dribble some dish soap on the bottom of the bowl. Pour some vinegar in a cup or bowl and give the kids each a syringe. Squirt baking soda dinosaur eggs to start them hatching and see the chemical reaction.

Ingredients:
Baking soda
Water
Food coloring
Syringes
White vinegar
Medium size container
Dish soap
Dinosaur toys
Parchment paper
Rubber gloves
Safety glasses

Project Extensions:

● Using a digital thermometer explore whether the chemical reaction is exothermic (releases heat) or endothermic (absorbs heat).

● Carefully place paper on the resulting liquid to create beautiful swirly art.

● Use the same reaction to fire Bottle Rockets.

Apple Scientific Method

Use the scientific method to answer the classic question, why do apples turn brown?

WATER   SALT   LEMON JUICE   CONTROL

HONEY   VITAMIN C   BUBBLE WATER   SPRITE

by Anne Carey **Left Brain Craft Brain**

Difficulty: ● ● ● ●

Estimated Project Time: 45 minutes

What's the STEAM behind it?

Why do apples turn brown? They're essentially rusting in a process called oxidation. Once the apple is cut or bruised, oxygen in the air combines with iron in the apple to form iron oxides which gives it the brown tint. Enzymes in the fruit (like polyphenol oxidase) make this process go faster. The oxidation process is also what causes metals to rust.

The browning of apples can be reduced by slowing oxidation in three different ways. 1) Cook the apples. 2) Reduce the exposure to oxygen. or 3) Reduce the pH of the fruit. Doing both 2 and 3 by covering apples with an acidic liquid is the best way to keep them from turning brown without cooking.

Ingredients:

Honey
Lemon juice
Salt
Vitamin C
Lemon-lime soda
Carbonated water
Tap water
Apple
8 small cups, jars, or ramekins
Paper and pen

 S T E A M

Instructions:

This experiment uses the Scientific Method to find the tastiest and most effective methods for reducing oxidation of apples. Go to page 15 for a full explanation of the Scientific Method.

Ask a Question: What is the best way to prevent apples from turning brown?

Do Research: Check out the science behind apples turning brown on page 42.

Make a Hypothesis: Guess which acidic solution will keep the apples the whitest and taste the best.

Design an Experiment: Submerge cut apple pieces in 7 different solutions and observe how well they work and how good they taste.

Make the Test Solutions

1. Honey: Dissolve 1 teaspoon honey in 1 cup water.
2. Lemon juice: Mix 1 teaspoon lemon juice and 1 cup water.
3. Salt: Dissolve 1/4 teaspoon salt in 1 cup water.
4. Vitamin C: Crush 1 tablet vitamin C and dissolve in 1 cup water.
5. Lemon-lime soda
6. Carbonated water (bubble water)
7. Tap water
8. Control: no solution

Prepare the Test Environment

1. Gather the test containers and label each with a test solution name.
2. Pour each test liquid into the appropriately labelled container.
3. Cut the apple into 8 pieces.
4. Place one apple slice in each test container and start a timer.

Record and Analyze Data

1. Check the apple pieces after five minutes or when the control apple slice is significantly brown.
2. Pour off solutions, inspect the apples and record observations for level of brown color.
3. Then taste each apple piece and record observations on taste.

Draw a Conclusion:

Review the data and answer the question "What is the best way to prevent apples from turning brown?"

Project Extensions:

- Take the experiment further by testing with different types of apples. Does using tarter apples change the conclusion?

- Make applesauce and test the first method of oxidation prevention - cooking the apples.

Kitchen Bubbles

Experiment to find out which kitchen tool blows the best bubbles.

by Jamie Hand **Kids STEAM Lab**

Ingredients:

**Bubble solution
(see page 52 for recipe)
Large tray or
shallow container
Variety of kitchen tools
Pipe cleaners**

Difficulty: ●

Estimated Project Time: 15 minutes

What's the STEAM behind it?

Bubbles are formed when air is trapped within a thin layer of water that is between two layers of soap (like a soap sandwich). Each soap molecule is oriented so that its water-loving (hydrophilic), head faces towards the trapped water layer. The hydrophobic (water-fearing) heads of the soap molecules face outwards. Because these hydrophobic heads are kind of greasy, they don't evaporate as quickly, giving the bubble extra life.

A bubble pops when the water between the soap layers evaporates.

 S T E A M

Instructions:

1. Pour bubble solution into a large tray or container.

2. Gather different kitchen tools that might be able to blow bubbles (whisk, spatula, fork, etc.)

3. Predict which objects you think will blow the best bubbles.

4. Test the objects! Try out each tool or object to see if your prediction was right.

5. What tool blows the largest bubble? What tool blows the smallest bubbles?

6. How does a kitchen tool compare to using a traditional bubble wand?

7. Use pipe cleaners to design and build your own bubble wand.

8. How does your bubble wand design compare to a kitchen tool?

Project Extensions:

- Research and test different recipes of bubble solution to see which recipe makes the best bubbles or experiment with creating your own bubble recipe.

- For more bubble fun, try Bubble Painting or a Bubble Lava Lamp.

Um el Tuweisat Game

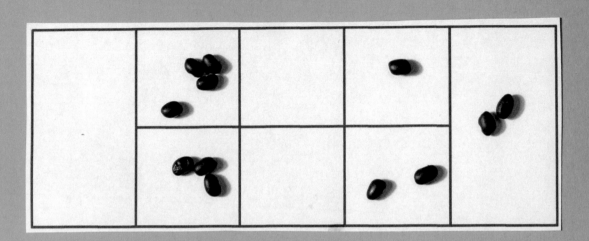

Um el Tuweisat is a traditional mancala game from Sudan.

by Erica Clark **What Do We Do All Day?**

Ingredients:

Paper
Pen
Ruler
12 large seeds
or dried beans
Two players

Difficulty: ● ● ●

Estimated Project Time: 15 minutes

What's the STEAM behind it?

Um el Tuweisat is an abstract strategy game, which means that game play has internal logic. There are no chance elements as there are in card or dice games. Players must use critical thinking, advance planning and engage logic skills in order to succeed. These skills are key components in STEAM fields, particularly engineering and math.

S T E **A** M

Instructions:

Game objective: to capture as many of your opponent's beans as possible.

1. Using ruler, paper and pen, draw a game board as shown in the photo or use the template on page 130.

2. Place 2 beans in each of 6 middle spaces of board.

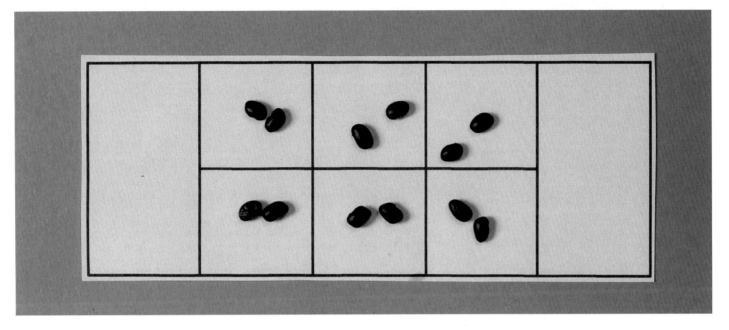

1. Players sit on opposite sides of the game board. The three squares on each player's side are "his squares." The empty rectangle to each player's right is his "home."

2. Player 1 begins by picking up two beans from any of his squares and "sowing" them by dropping them into consecutive squares. Do not drop any beans into a home space.

3. Beans picked up from the right hand square are sown to the right. Beans picked up from the left hand square are sown to the left. Beans picked up from the center square can be sown in either direction.

4. If the last bean drops into a square on your opponent's side bringing the total in that square to 2 beans, you capture the beans in that square and place them in your home. In addition, if, when capturing, there are 2 beans in the square just behind you (going backwards in the direction you were sowing) then you capture those beans, too.

5. Play continues until one player has no beans left on his side of the game board.

6. The player with the most beans in his home wins.

Project Extensions:

- Um el Tuweisat is a game of transfer in the mancala family. There are dozens of mancala variations played around the world. Kids who enjoyed Um el Tuweisat can research other mancala variations to try.
- Add an artistic component to gaming by creating a custom board out of wood or craft supplies.
- To keep playing, try these other games. Tchuka Ruma is a solitary mancala type game. Dara is another abstract strategy game from Africa.

Secret Messages

Write a secret message that can only be deciphered by a chemical reaction called oxidation.

Difficulty: ●●

by Amber Scardino **Figment Creative Labs**

Estimated Project Time: 25 minutes

What's the STEAM behind it?

These secret messages appear because of a chemical reaction called oxidation. Colorless carbon-based compounds in the lemon juice absorb into the paper as the design is created. When the paper is heated, the carbon in the lemon juice releases. Then, when the carbon mixes with oxygen, it undergoes oxidation and turns brown. This is the same process that causes apples to turn brown on page 42. The depth of tone of the brown design is dependent upon how much lemon juice is applied to the paper.

Ingredients:

Lemon
Small bowl
Cup
Cotton swabs
Paper
Baking sheet
Oven

Instructions:

1. Squeeze lemon juice into a small bowl.

2. Place a sheet of paper on a baking sheet.

3. Dip a cotton swab in juice. Write a secret message on paper or draw a picture. It will disappear as it dries.

4. To reveal the message, preheat oven to 400 degrees and bake for 15 minutes.

Project Extensions:

● Draw a treasure map and send someone on a treasure hunt. Or give clues to a mystery to be solved.

● Check out how secret messages make great Valentines too!

 **S** T E A M

Apple Print Math Patterns

Make patterns using this fun art technique of printing with apples!

by Chelsey Marashian **Buggy & Buddy**

Difficulty: ●

Estimated Project Time: 20 minutes

What's the STEAM behind it?

In this activity kids use the art technique of stamping to explore the insides of an apple. The apple is a fruit - a product of a tree or plant that contains seeds, flesh, skin, and a stem. Stamping is also a perfect project for perfecting patterns, critical elements to early math skill development.

Instructions:

1. Gather the apples together and observe them closely. What do you notice? How do they feel, smell, look? Before cutting the apples in half, predict what they will look like inside.

2. Have an adult cut the apples in half vertically. Observe the inside of the apples. Were the predictions correct?

3. Place different colors of tempera paint onto each paper plate.

4. Hold the apple half from top to bottom rather than on the sides (to get a good grip) and dip and rub the apple around in the paint. Now press the apple onto paper to make an apple print.

5. Use the different apple halves and colors of paint to create a math pattern on your strip of paper.

6. Make different patterns on other strips of paper. How many different patterns can you make?

7. When the paint is dry, use markers or crayons to draw a stem and leaves on the apple prints.

Ingredients:

Various apples
Knife
Tempera paint in various colors
White construction paper
Paper plates
Markers (optional)
Paper (optional)

Project Extensions:

● Explore how apple prints change when the apple is cut horizontally instead of vertically. Then staple your apple print papers into a pattern book.

● For another nature art activity, explore Leaf and Flower Pounding.

 S T E A M

Dancing Rice

Make rice dance with science!

by Chelsey Marashian **Buggy & Buddy**

Difficulty: ●●
Estimated Project Time: 15 minutes

Ingredients:
Clear cup or container
Water
Baking soda
Vinegar
Measuring cups
Measuring spoons
Spoon
Rice
Food coloring
(optional)

Project Extensions:

● Compare different types of rice or raisins or lentils. Do they all dance? Why or why not? How about in other liquids like soda or carbonated water? Or in waters of different temperatures.

● Explore whether objects Sink or Float in this fun experiment.

What's the STEAM behind it?

Explore the principle of density with this dancing rice experiment! When rice is first added to a baking soda and water mixture, it sinks to the bottom because the rice is more dense than the mixture. When vinegar is added the baking soda and vinegar react to form a gas, carbon dioxide. The bubbles of carbon dioxide then adhere to rice at the bottom of the cup. As bubbles of carbon dioxide adhere to the rice the density of the rice is lowered, causing it to rise to the surface. Once it reaches the surface, the gas is released, and the rice falls back down again.

Incorporate art by adding various colors of food coloring to your mixture. Watch them mix and swirl and create new colors!

Instructions:

1. Pour one cup of water into a clear cup.

2. Add 1 teaspoon of baking soda to the water and stir.

3. Sprinkle rice into the mixture. Watch what happens to the rice. The rice should sink to the bottom of the cup. (If the rice doesn't sink, it might be less dense than the mixture. Try a different kind of rice, broken pieces of spaghetti, or raisins.)

4. Add 1 tablespoon of vinegar to the water. Tiny bubbles should start to form on the rice.

5. Observe what happens over the next few minutes. The rice will begin rising to the surface. Once it reaches the top, it will fall down again to the bottom of the cup.

6. Optional: Add a couple drops of food coloring and watch it slowly begin to mix into the solution.

7. As the rising and falling of the rice slows, add more baking soda and watch what happens. Try adding more vinegar. Does the rice continue to dance?

8. If you are using a larger container, be sure to use larger amounts of baking soda and vinegar.

S T E A M

Play Dough

Ingredients:

- **1 cup water**
- **1 cup flour**
- **1/2 cup salt**
- **1 Tbsp oil (coconut or canola)**
- **1 Tbsp cream of tartar**
- **Food coloring**

Instructions:

1. Combine all ingredients in a large saucepan. Stir to combine.

2. Heat saucepan over medium heat stirring constantly.

3. After about 3-5 minutes the playdough should start to form a solid mass. Once it pulls away from the sides of the pan and forms a ball, it is ready.

4. Remove the pan from heat, place the dough into a large bowl and let cool.

5. Store the dough in an airtight container.

The classic play recipe!

Oobleck

Ingredients:

- **2 cups cornstarch**
- **1 cup water**
- **Food coloring (optional)**

Instructions:

1. Pour 2 cups cornstarch into a bowl

2. Add 1 cup of water and stir to combine

3. If adding food coloring to your oobleck do it at the mixing stage

What's the STEAM behind it?

Oobleck is a non-Newtonian fluid, a fancy name for a material that changes viscosity (thickness) with pressure. Give it a hard push, it feels solid. Be more gentle, and it flows like a liquid. Oobleck and slime are examples of shear-thickening non-Newtonian fluids, meaning they get thicker with more pressure. Nail polish and ketchup are examples of shear thinning non-Newtonian fluids, meaning they get thinner with pressure.

Easy sensory science!

Fizzing Dough

Ingredients:

- 1 cup baking soda
- 4 tablespoons water
- Food coloring (optional)
- Reactors to test:
- Vinegar
- Lemon juice
- Vinegar and dish soap

Instructions:

1. In a bowl, mix baking soda and water until you have a crumbly dough.

2. If you want your dough to be colored, add a small amount of food coloring to your water before mixing with the baking soda.

3. Mold the dough into shapes using cookie cutters, or balls using your hands.

4. Test what liquid causes the biggest fizzing reaction by adding the liquids to your dough one at a time.

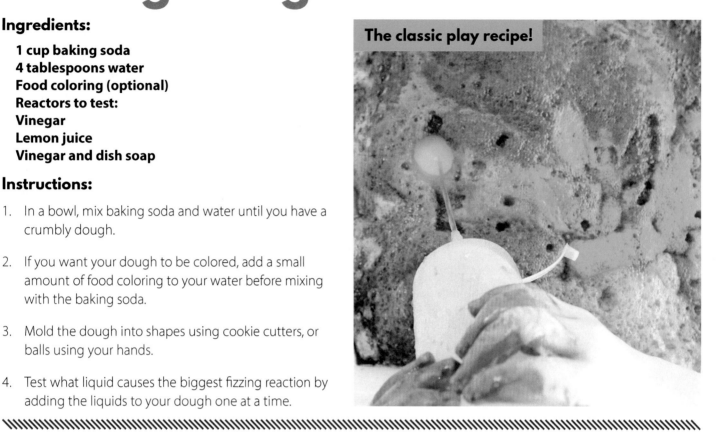

The classic play recipe!

Bubble Solution

Ingredients:

- 6 cups water
- 1/2 cup cornstarch
- 1/2 cup dish detergent (like Dawn)
- 1 tbsp baking powder
- 1 tbsp glycerin

Instructions:

1. Make the solution the day before planning to use it to allow it to thicken.

2. Mix water and cornstarch together until cornstarch is dissolved.

3. Add in dish detergent, baking powder, and glycerin slowly and mix.

4. Let the solution rest to thicken before using.

The best bubble recipe!

Colored Counting Beans

Ingredients:

1 bag of lightly colored beans like lima or white
Food coloring
Zipper bags (1 per color)
Paper towels
Trays or plates

Instructions:

1. For each color, measure 1 cup of beans and pour into a zipper bag.

2. Add 20 drops of food coloring. Seal the bag closed tightly.

3. Shake well for about 30 seconds or until the food coloring is well dispersed and no white spots are left on the beans.

4. Place paper towels on trays or plates and pour out beans onto paper towels. Keep colors separated until the beans dry, about 4-6 hours.

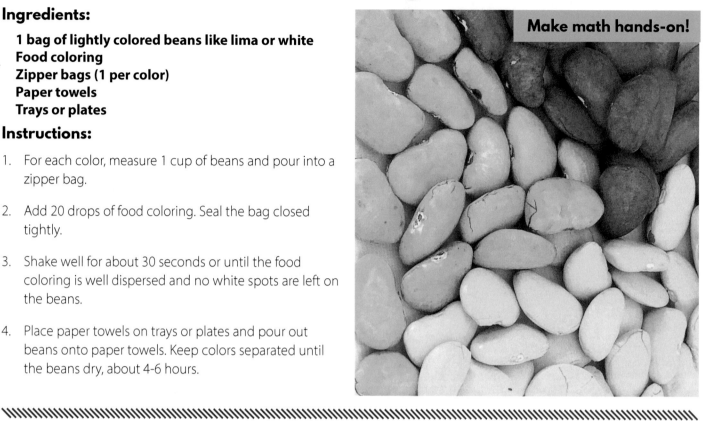

Make math hands-on!

Cloud Dough

Ingredients:

2 cups flour
1/4 cup canola or other mild vegetable oil
Candy coloring (optional)

Instructions:

Because cloud dough is oil based, standard food coloring won't work, but candy coloring will.

1. Add 2 cups flour to a large bowl.

2. Mix 1/4 cup of oil with 1 tsp candy food coloring, stir.

3. Add the colored oil to the flour; stir to combine.

4. Knead the dough with your hands to fully distribute color and oil.

Like building with clouds!

Taste-Safe Slime

Ingredients:

- 1 cup water
- Food coloring (optional)
- 3 tablespoons Metamucil Free Fiber Supplement
- Large microwavable bowl
- Microwave

Instructions:

1. Pour water slowly into large microwaveable bowl. Add food coloring if desired. Add Metamucil and stir well.

2. Microwave on high for 5 minutes. Do not walk away from microwave! Make sure it does not overflow the bowl.

3. Stir and continue to cook on high for 30 second increments until the slime gets to the right slimy texture.

4. Remove from microwave with hot pads and let cool until room temperature.

Borax-free slime!

Salt Dough

Ingredients:

- 4 cups flour
- 1 cup salt
- 1 1/2 cups warm water

Instructions:

1. Preheat oven to 300 degrees F.

2. Mix together flour and salt in small bowl.

3. Add water a little at a time and mix. Continue mixing until all water is incorporated and dough looks uniform.

4. Place on floured surface and knead well.

5. Roll out dough and use cookie cutters to make shapes.

6. Place shapes on a cookie sheet and bake for 2 hours, or until hard.

Perfect for keepsakes!

Glowing Waterbeads

Ingredients:

Clear waterbeads
Vitamin B-2 (riboflavin) capsule
Water
Large plastic container with lid
UV light (blacklight)

Instructions:

1. Add 1 tablespoon clear waterbeads and 1 gallon of water into plastic container.

2. Empty one vitamin B-2 capsule into the water and mix.

3. Cover container and let sit until beads are full size, about 12 hours.

4. Go in a dark area and turn on UV light. Play!

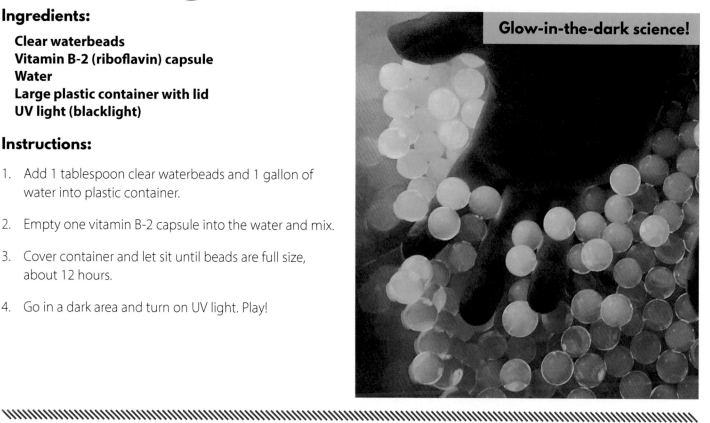

Glow-in-the-dark science!

Marshmallow Dough

Ingredients:

5 large marshmallows
3 tablespoons cornstarch
1 tablespoon icing or powdered sugar
1 tablespoon coconut opil
Food coloring

Instructions:

1. In a bowl mix 3 tablespoons of cornstarch with 1 tablespoon of icing sugar. Set to the side.

2. In a microwave safe container place 5 marshmallows, plus a tablespoon of coconut oil and a few drops of food colouring.

3. Microwave marshmallow mixture in 30 second increments & never take your eyes off of it. Stir between increments and continue heating until marshmallows and coconut oil are melted.

4. Mix melted marshmallows until they form a ball.

5. Place marshmallow ball in the cornstarch/icing sugar mixture. Mix a little and let it sit for a few seconds to cool, then lift it out with your hands and start kneading it. If it feels a bit sticky, press it into your cornstarch mixture, then work it again.

Sweet, creative fun!

COLOR

Rainbow Rubber Eggs

A classic science project with a colorful twist!

by Ana Dziengel **Babble Dabble Do**

Difficulty: ● ● ● ● ●

Estimated Project Time: 20 minutes

What's the STEAM behind it?

Vinegar is an acid and it dissolves the eggshell which is made from calcium carbonate, just like chalk. Calcium carbonate and acetic acid (vinegar) create a chemical reaction which produces carbon dioxide, those are the bubbles forming around the shell. Eventually the entire shell is dissolved leaving the rubbery egg membrane beneath it exposed.

Once the shell is dissolved the rubbery egg is translucent, meaning light shines through, but details can not be seen through it. Many artists use translucency in their work to layer colors and create depth. Light & Space was an art movement in the 1960s where artists explored light and color using a variety of translucent materials.

Ingredients:

Eggs
Clear cup or jar (1 per egg)
Distilled white vinegar
Food coloring
Bowl of water

  S T E A M

Instructions:

1. Carefully place a raw egg in a clear jar or cup.

2. Pour enough vinegar in the cup to completely submerge the egg.

3. Add in a few generous drops of food coloring and stir gently. Make a rubber egg for each color of the rainbow.

4. Wait. Observe the egg each day. The vinegar will begin to dissolve the eggshell over the course of several days and as it dissolves it will begin to bubble.

5. After about 3-5 days remove the egg from the vinegar and place it in a bowl of water.

6. Gently rub away the shell to reveal the membrane that lies just below it.

7. Bounce the egg…but not too hard! The egg will now be bouncy and rubbery but it is still raw on the inside. Press it and bounce to test just how rubbery it is but beware, it will still break! Make sure to break at least one to see what the egg looks like inside!

Project Extensions:

 Try adding a piece of chalk to the jar along with the egg and vinegar. Does it speed up or slow down the chemical reaction between the acetic acid and calcium carbonate?

 Make pickled eggs! Acetic acid is also used to pickle foods because it prevents bacteria growth. Did you know that pickling eggs will keep them edible for up to 3-4 months? Find a safe recipe online and follow the instructions to make an edible version of this science project!

 Experiment with translucency in this <u>Stained Glass Pasta</u> art project

Salt Painting

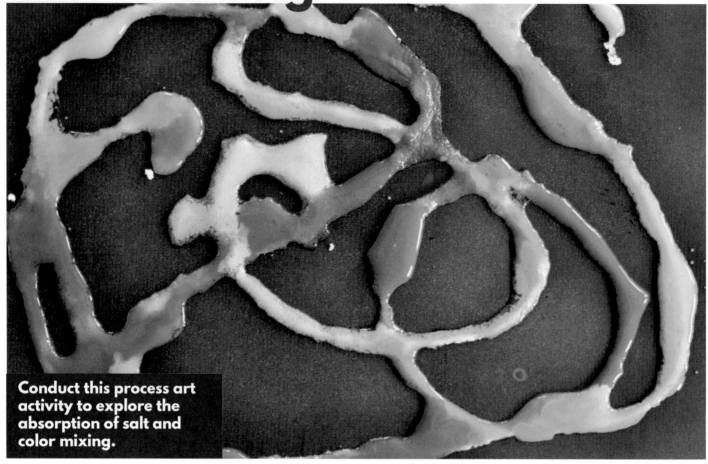

Conduct this process art activity to explore the absorption of salt and color mixing.

by Jamie Hand **Kids STEAM Lab**

Ingredients:
Salt
Glue bottle
Black cardstock paper
Bowl
Tray
Liquid watercolors
or food coloring
Pipette
Digital camera or smart
phone (optional)

Difficulty:

Estimated Project Time: 20 minutes

What's the STEAM behind it?

Salt is a natural mineral made up of sodium and chlorine. Salt absorbs water because it is highly attracted to water molecules. In this activity the drops of watercolor are absorbed by the salt., causing it to appear to move down the lines.

 S T E A M

Instructions:

1. Use the glue bottle to draw a design on the black paper.

2. Sprinkle salt over the entire paper covering your glue design. Shake off the excess salt into a bowl.

3. Drip drops of color onto the salt using the pipette. What happens to the colors as they are absorbed by the salt? What happens when two different colors mix on the salt?

4. Take a digital photograph to document and record the finished work of art as the salt will eventually flake off.

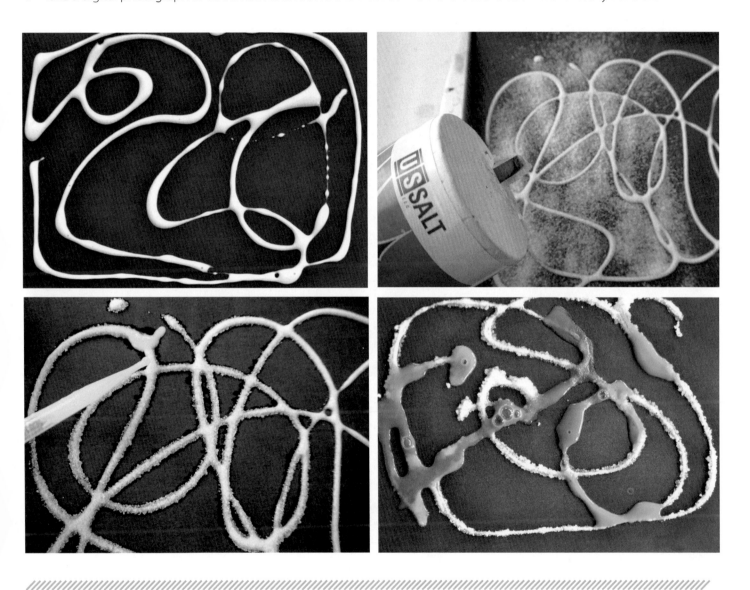

Project Extensions:

- Paint a picture using watercolor paint. While the paint is still wet, sprinkle salt onto the paint. What happens to the color?

- For another fun salt project, try creating with Homemade Salt Dough.

Cabbage Juice Science

Make your own pH indicator with cabbage!

milk

Rubbing Alcohol

Shampoo

Windex

Lemon Juice

Coconut Water

Diet Coke

V8 Juice

by Karyn Tripp **Teach Beside Me**

Difficulty: ●●●

Estimated Project Time: 30 minutes

What's the STEAM behind it?

Cabbage water has a substance in it called anthocyanin. It is a pH indicator that changes color when acids or bases are added to it. With an acid, it will turn red and with a base it will turn green. If it is neutral the color will not change.

Ingredients:

**Head of red cabbage
Ingredients for
testing the pH:
Milk
Rubbing alcohol
Ammonia or
window cleaner
Lemon juice
Coke
Tomato juice
Baking soda**

Instructions:

1. Chop up half of a head of red cabbage.

2. Place in a large pot and cover with water.

3. Boil on the stove until the cabbage is tender and the water is a dark purple color.

4. Drain the cabbage, saving the water. (You can use the cabbage in a soup or other recipes!)

5. Let the water cool and pour into several small containers.

6. Pour a small amount of the various liquids into the different cups to see the reaction. Different liquids will turn the cabbage water different colors.

Project Extensions:

- You can try this experiment with blueberries and purple grape juice too!

- Save the extra cabbage juice for the Green Eggs on page 108 or Unicorn Noodles on page 104.

S T E A M

Magic Milk

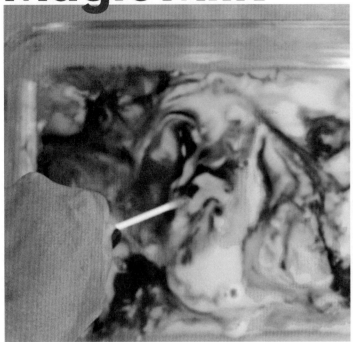

Make the color swirl with a simple science magic trick.

by Ana Dziengel **Babble Dabble Do**

Difficulty:

Estimated Project Time: 10 minutes

What's the STEAM behind it?

The molecules in dish soap are attracted to the fat molecules in the milk. When soap is introduced to the milk, the molecules race around trying to bond. The food coloring gets pushed around in the process and appears to burst. Eventually the soap and fat molecules bond and the reaction stops.

The magic milk experiment creates beautiful swirls of color that look like the art technique called marbling. Marbling is a form of art in which color is mixed on top of a liquid and the pattern is preserved by carefully laying paper or fabric on the surface to capture a print.

Ingredients:

Almond milk or cow's milk
Dishsoap
Q-tips
Food coloring
Shallow plate or wide bowl

Instructions:

1. Add a thin layer of milk to a plate or bowl

2. Drop in at least 2 drops of each color of food coloring.

3. Generously dip the end of a Q-tip in dish soap.

4. Now dip a Q-tip into the milk next to a drop of color. The color will burst as soon as the dish soap hits it. It's a great effect but very short lived.

5. Gently swirl the q-tip through the milk and watch rivers of color start to form. Continue until the colors begin to mix and become brown. Empty your plate/bowl and repeat.

Project Extensions:

Experiment with different kinds of milk: skim, whole, 2%, almond, cashew, cow, rice, coconut. Which works best and why?

What happens if you limit yourself to using only primary colors? Will you see some secondary colors appear in the experiment?

Be sure to Preserve Your Milk Design on Paper.

    S T E A M

Candy Rainbows

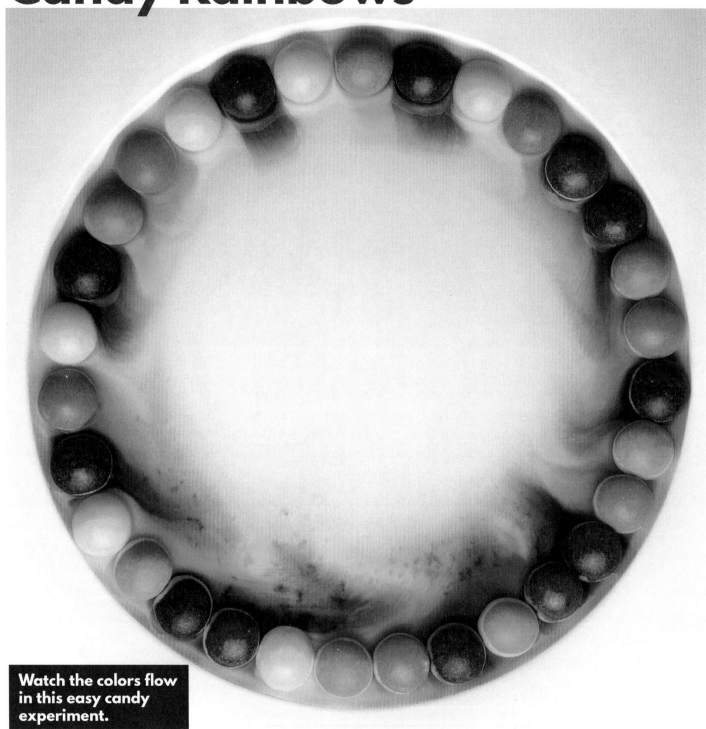

Watch the colors flow in this easy candy experiment.

by Anne Carey **Left Brain Craft Brain**

S T E A M

Ingredients:

**Colorful round candies
like Skittles, M&M's,
or Gobstoppers
Round shallow plate
Water**

Difficulty: ●
Estimated Project Time: 10 minutes

What's the STEAM behind it?

Candy such as Skittles & M&M's contain artificial colors called dyes that are easily dissolvable in water. As the dyes move into the water, they diffuse across the plate. The dye molecules want to travel to areas of lower concentration of dye from areas where there is a lot of dye. Eventually the colors reach equilibrium, where all the areas have equal concentrations of dye.

Instructions:

1. Arrange the candies in a circle around the outside of the plate.

2. Pour a small amount of water into the center of the plate. Use enough that all of the candies get wet on the bottom.

3. Watch the color patterns form!

4. Repeat with another pattern of candy. How did the colors change?

Project Extensions:

● Make candy paint by placing a few candies of each color in individual jars or wells of a paint palette. Add water, let them dissolve for about an hour, and then paint.

● Try using only primary colored candy and watch the color mixing happen. Does it make secondary colors?

● Look for the S's or M's that float off the candy!

● For more candy science try this Candy Chromatography Experiment.

Coffee Paint

Use an unexpected paint to learn about tone and value.

by Amber Scardino **Figment Creative Labs**

Difficulty: ● ●

Estimated Project Time: 30 minutes

What's the STEAM behind it?

Ever wonder why coffee is brown? Coffee beans are green before they are roasted but get their dark toasty shade from something called the Maillard Reaction. Simple sugars and amino acids in the coffee beans react at high temperatures to become polymers called melanoidins. These polymers turn the coffee brown.

This is an art method that shows gradations in value, depending on how much you use of one ingredient. Value refers to the lightness or darkness of a color.

Ingredients:
Watercolor paper
Pencil
4 jars
4 paint brushes
Instant coffee
(Normal coffee grounds will not work.)
Warm water
Measuring spoons:
1 Tbsp, ½ tsp, ¼ tsp.

S T E A M

Instructions:

Make the Coffee Paint:

1. Add equal amounts of warm water to each jar.

2. Add coffee to the jars and stir. Feel free to play with these amounts to get the desired gradation.
   - Jar #1: 2 Tbsp. coffee
   - Jar #2: 1 Tbsp. coffee
   - Jar #3: ½ tsp. coffee
   - Jar #4: ¼ tsp. coffee

Make your Painting:

1. First make a tone sample by drawing stripes of each jar of paint. How do they differ?

1. Draw a picture on watercolor paper lightly using a pencil.

2. Start painting with the lightest paint (jar #4). Continue adding shading with the other paints, lightest to darkest.

Project Extensions:

- Try this project with tea or juice, too.

- Try different drawings and play around with different measurements.

- What can you turn your tone samples into? How about some people or chocolate bars?

Walking Water

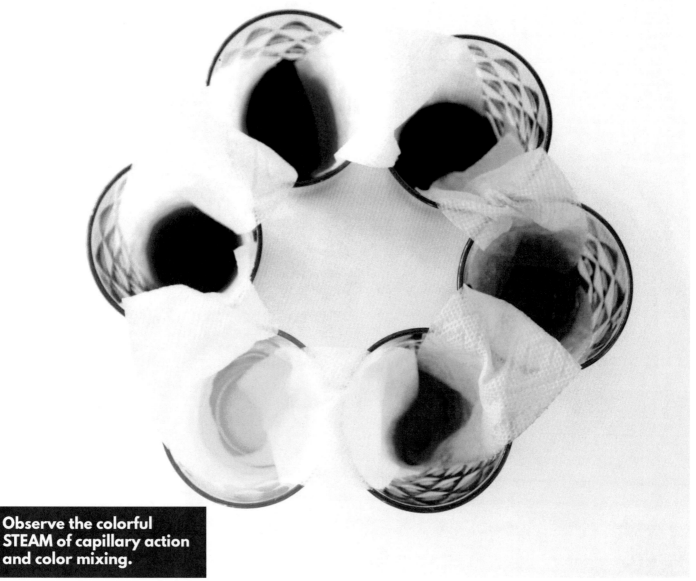

Observe the colorful STEAM of capillary action and color mixing.

by Erica Clark **What Do We Do All Day?**

Ingredients:

4 paper towels
Water
Food coloring:
red, yellow and blue
5 glass jars
or glasses

Difficulty: ● ●

Estimated Project Time: 10 minutes prep,
several hours to one day for
observation

S T E A M

What's the STEAM behind it?

The colored water "walks" from jar to jar due to capillary action. The forces of cohesion, surface tension and adhesion work to move water from one location to another. Cohesion means water molecules stay close to each other, adhesion means they stick to each other, and surface tension means water molecules have the ability to stick to other surfaces. These three forces work together to make water a "sticky" substance that can travel porous surfaces, even against the force of gravity. When two different primary colors mix together in the empty jar, they form a secondary color.

Plants use capillary action to "drink" water through up through their roots. Capillary action is the reason paper towels can absorb liquids.

Instructions:

1. Fill 3 glass jars full with water. Add red food coloring to one jar, yellow to the second, and blue to the third.

2. Line up glass jars. Alternate full jars with empty jars. Red-empty-yellow-empty-blue.

3. Fold four paper towels lengthwise in thirds. Place one end of the first paper towel in the jar with red water, place the second end of the same towel the the empty jar just next to it. Repeat so that each jar holds two ends of towel. The jars at either end of the line will only contain one paper towel. Alternatively, you can place the jars in a circle.

4. Over the next several hours (it may take as long as a few days, depending upon the climate) observe how the water "walks" from the full jars to the empty jars. Note how the colors combine to create new colors.

Project Extensions:

- Experiment with plants to see how capillary action works in nature. Place white daisies, celery, or cabbage leaves in jars filled with colored water and note how over time they change color. For extra fun, slice the stems and place each half of each stem in a different color.

- For more water experimentation, try these Water Drop Races.

   S T E A M

Homemade Paint

Experiment to create your own homemade paint recipe.

by Jamie Hand **Kids STEAM Lab**

Ingredients:
(makes one color)
1 Tbsp. flour
1 Tbsp. salt
1 Tbsp. liquid dish soap
2 Tbsp. water
Small bowl
Food coloring
Paint brush
Paper

Difficulty:

Estimated Project Time: 20 minutes

What's the STEAM behind it?

Store bough paint is made up of three elements: pigment, binder and the solvent. The pigment is the color of the paint. The binder helps the pigment stick to the art surface. The solvent helps dissolve the pigment and binder so that it is easier to spread or flow across your surface. In this recipe, the water, flour, and salt serve as a binder. The soap helps the paint flow.

S T E A M

Instructions:

1. In a small bowl, mix together flour, salt and liquid dish soap.

2. Slowly add up to 2 T of water and stir gently. Too thin? Add more flour. Too thick? Add more water.

3. Add several drops of food coloring to the bowl. Stir well.

4. Repeat as needed for each desired color.

5. Grab some paper and a brush and paint!

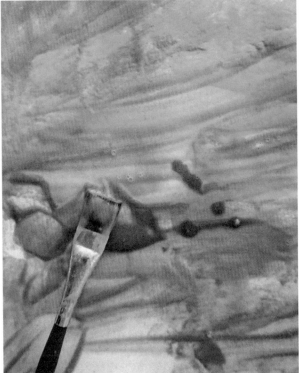

Project Extensions:

- How many new colors can you create using the primary colors: red, yellow and blue?

- Make Homemade Watercolor Sparkle Paint, too!

Pasta Suncatchers

Explore both art and math patterns in this colorful pasta project.

by Ana Dziengel **Babble Dabble Do**

Difficulty: ● ●

Estimated Project Time: 15 minutes to make, several days drying time

Ingredients:

Pasta (variety of shapes and sizes)
Food coloring
Rubbing alcohol
Ziploc baggies
Paper towels
Recycled plastic lids
Glue

What's the STEAM behind it?

This project explores patterns, a concept present in both math and art. A pattern as defined in art is an organizing structure for a composition. Patterns typically repeat in drawings and designs. Try gluing your pasta to the lid to form patterns, like a mandala, a circular, abstract design.

A pattern or sequence in math is an ordered set of numbers or objects that follow a certain rule. Try making some sequenced patterns in the suncatchers such as placing several pastas shapes of one color down, then adding another color, then repeating again with the first color.

S T E **A** **M**

Instructions:

Dye the Pasta:

1. In a large ziploc bag add 1 teaspoon of rubbing alcohol, a generous squeeze of food coloring, and a few handfuls of pasta.

2. Knead the bag to distribute the color evenly to all the pasta pieces. Let sit for 10-15 minutes in the bag, then empty the pasta onto paper towels and let dry for a few hours.

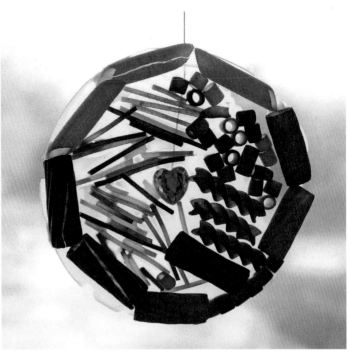

Make the Suncatchers:

1. Pour glue in the bottom of a lid. The more glue, the more sturdy your final suncatcher will be.

2. Add the dry colored pasta. Make patterns and designs using the different shapes.

3. Let the glue dry. Depending on how much glue you used, these will take a few days to completely dry.

4. When dry, pop your suncatcher out of the lid and hang it in a window! Be sure to use heavy-duty tape, such as duct tape, when hanging these! They are heavy and will shatter if dropped.

Project Extensions:

- Challenge kids to create designs with a secret code! Assign different pasta shapes and colors a corresponding letter, then ask kids to spell their name in code using the assigned shapes.

- After a design is finished, play a math guessing game. Ask kids to estimate how many shapes of one type of pasta they used, then go back and have them count to see how close their estimate was.

- Explore more Math Art with String Art Geometry or 3-D Geometric Shapes

S T E A M

GROW

Gelatin Printmaking

Gelatin printmaking is a fun hands-on way to explore monoprinting without fancy equipment.

by Jamie Hand **Kids STEAM Lab**

Difficulty: ● ● ● ● ●

Estimated Project Time: 15 minutes +
60 minutes gelatin set time +
60 minutes drying time

Ingredients:

8 envelopes gelatin powder
2 cups hot water
2 cups glycerin
9" x 13" Pan with
Smooth-bottom bowl
Knife
Cookie sheet or tray
Washable paint
Brayer (or smooth paint
roller)
Cotton swab
White paper
Baby wipe

What's the STEAM behind it?

Gelatin printmaking is a form of monoprinting. This process recreates unique designs each time you create a print. So each picture is one of a kind. This is different from other printmaking methods where you can make multiple copies of a single design.

Gelatin makes a firm surface for printing due to its polymer makeup. When liquid is added to the gelatin, it blooms by forming a triple helix polymer chain with the liquid interspersed throughout.

S T E A M

Instructions:

Make the Gelatin Printing Plate

1. Pour 2 cups of glycerin in a bowl and sprinkle in 8 packages of gelatin. Stir gently.

2. Add 2 cups of boiling water. Gently stir until the gelatin has dissolved.

3. Slowly, pour the gelatin mixture into a pan. Allow the gelatin to completely set for at least one hour.

4. Use a knife to loosen the gelatin around the edges of the pan and slide out the gelatin plate. Place the gelatin upside down on a cookie sheet.

Printmaking on a Gelatin Plate

1. Squirt paint onto the gelatin printing plate. Roll out the paint with the brayer.

2. Use a cotton swab to gently draw a design in the paint.

3. Place a white sheet of paper over the top of your paint and rub firmly on top of the paper. Lift to reveal your the print.

4. To make another print, add more paint and create a new design. If necessary, clean the gelatin printing plate by wiping with a baby wipe.

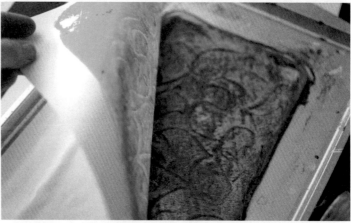

Project Extensions:

- What other ways can you create a monoprint with a gelatin plate? Try using different tools to draw a design.

- Also try making Precise Gelatin Prints Using Stencils.

Strawberry DNA

See DNA with the naked eye in this strawberry experiment.

by Karyn Tripp **Teach Beside Me**

Difficulty: ● ● ●

Estimated Project Time: 20 minutes

What's the STEAM behind it?

All living things have DNA. When scientists want to study the DNA of something, they have to extract it. This experiment follows this process. The soap helps pop the cell open and the alcohol causes the DNA to separate. The salt bonds to the DNA and separates it from the water.

The DNA of a strawberry is easy to extract and examine because each strawberry cell has eight copies of the genome. Most living organisms have just one per cell. A typical strand of DNA is too small to see with your eyes, but this extraction liquid clumps the cells together making it easier to see.

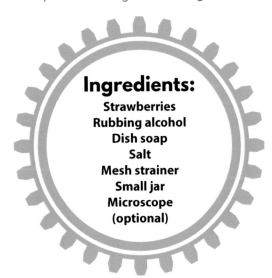

Ingredients:
Strawberries
Rubbing alcohol
Dish soap
Salt
Mesh strainer
Small jar
Microscope
(optional)

Instructions:

1. Chill a bottle of rubbing alcohol in the fridge or freezer.

2. Create the DNA extraction liquid by mixing 1/3 c. water, 2 teaspoons of dish soap, and ¼ teaspoon of salt.

3. Remove the leaves of a strawberry and place the strawberry in a ziploc bag.

4. Add DNA extraction soap mixture to the bag and seal tightly, removing excess air.

5. Mash the strawberry until there are no large pieces remaining.

6. Pour the strawberry mixture through a strainer keeping the liquid, but not the pulp. Press out all the liquid.

7. Pour strawberry liquid into a small jar and add 2 teaspoons of cold rubbing alcohol. There will be a separation of materials with a white clump of material on top. That is the DNA of the strawberry.

8. Examine under a microscope!

Project Extensions:

● Try extracting the DNA of other foods like onions, apples, kiwis, etc. using the same method.

    S T E A M

Seed Studies

Dissect fruit to reveal the seeds inside. Then create!

by Leslie Manlapig **Pink Stripey Socks**

Difficulty: ● ●

Estimated Project Time: 10 minutes

What's the STEAM behind it?

Fruit develops from the ovaries of flowers. The outer layers of the fruits help to protect and disperse the seeds inside. If given the proper environment, these seeds can eventually grow to create more plants and more fruit.

Instructions:

1. Cut open the fruit with a knife with adult supervision.

2. Look around for the seeds and carefully remove them from the fruit.

3. Compare and contrast the seeds. How are they different? Similar?

4. Dry off the seeds for the art project.

5. Create paper collages of the fruit. Glue your seeds onto your artwork to give it a scientific touch!

Ingredients:

Different types of fruit
Knives
Scissors
Paper towels
Paper in assorted colors
Glue stick

Project Extensions:

● For another project using fruit, check out the Apple Prints on page 61.

Wheatgrass on Waterbeads

Watch the plant life cycle happen with quick-growing seeds.

by Anne Carey **Left Brain Craft Brain**

S T E A M

Ingredients:

Clear waterbeads
Water
Clear vase or jar
Wheatgrass seeds
Ruler
Paper
Sharpie

Difficulty: ●

Estimated Project Time: 10 minute prep,
1 week growing time

What's the STEAM behind it?

Wheatgrass are the freshly grown leavs of the common wheat plant and it's a great seed to experience the plant life cycle because it grows so quickly. As the plants grow on the waterbeads, the seed, germination, and growth phases wil be visible. Germination is the sprouting of a seedling from the seed.

Instructions:

1. Pour 1 teaspoon of waterbeads into your vase and add water to about 2/3 full. Let them sit for 4-6 hours. If they seem to have run out of water, add more water and let them expand until they stop growing. Then drain off remaining water.

2. Sprinkle about 1 Tablespoon of wheatgrass seeds on top of the waterbeads. Place in a sunny spot and watch them grow. Identify the phases of the plant life cycle as they happen.

3. Measure the height of your grass each day and mark with a Sharpie on the side of the vase or on a piece of paper.

Project Extensions:

● Try growing other plants on water beads. Or change up the growing surface and grow seeds on cut sponges. You can create whatever shape you want with the sponges!

Grow Gummy Bears

Have you ever seen a gummy bear grow?

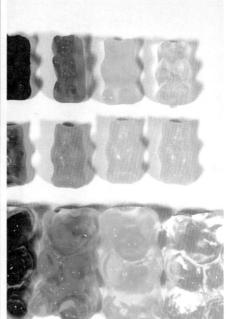

Difficulty: ●

Estimated Project Time: 6-8 hours

What's the STEAM behind it?

There are several cool science principles at play in these growing gummy bears. First is **Solubility**. Solubility is the ability for a liquid, solid, or gas to dissolve in a different liquid, solid, or gas. This experiment tests gummy bears' solubility in different solutions like salt and baking soda.

Also at work is something called **Osmosis**. Osmosis is the movement of molecules through a membrane to equalize concentrations of a substance on each side of the membrane. The gummy bear membrane is made of gelatin and things like salt and oil are the substances that need to come to equal concentrations inside the gummy bear and in the cup.

Ingredients:
Gummy bears
Clear cups or containers
Water
Vinegar
Oil
Baking soda
Salt

by Amber Scardino **Figment Creative Labs**

Instructions:

1. Add salt to boiling water until no more salt dissolves. Use caution and have an adult assist. Place salt solution in the refrigerator and allow to cool.

2. Repeat with baking soda and water.

3. Set out 6 cups and place a gummy bear in each cup. Don't add anything to the first cup, the control. In each of the other cups add one of the solutions: water, vinegar, oil, baking soda or salt water. Label each cup with the liquid used.

4. Make a hypothesis of what will happen to each gummy bear.

5. Let sit for 6 hours. Examine results and make a conclusion.

Project Extensions:

● Bring some math into this experiment by drawing a chart comparing the sizes and growth of the gummy bears.

● Melt the gummy bears down (if using different colored gummy bears) and make faux stained glass.

S T E A M

Fruit Enzymes

Explore enzymes in this fruity gelatin experiment.

by Karyn Tripp **Teach Beside Me**

Difficulty: ● ●

Estimated Project Time: 10 minutes for setup, several hours for gelatin to harden

What's the STEAM behind it?

Fruit contains enzymes, a substance created by a living organism to bring about a chemical reaction. This experiment tests the effects of the protein-digesting enzyme bromelain, which is often used as a meat tenderizer. DIfferent fruits contain different levels of bromelain enzyme.

Gelatin is made out of animal proteins. When water is added to the gelatin, long chains of protein form. Water gets trapped in the middle of these long chains, and turns the liquid into a semi-solid. Since the enzyme bromelain digests proteins, it eats away at the gelatin. The protein chains collapse, making everything watery again.

Ingredients:

Gelatin (plain or flavored)
Variety of cut fruit:
Pineapple
Kiwi
Orange
Strawberry
Several bowls
or petri dishes

Instructions:

1. Make the gelatin according to the package directions.

2. Add cut fruit into the different bowls or petri dishes, leaving one without fruit for the control.

3. Divide the gelatin among the bowls.

4. Refrigerate for a few hours to set.

5. Hypothesize about which fruits will react with the gelatin.

Project Extensions:

● Learn about bromeliads. Pineapples are bromeliads which are spiky plants that grow on the ground and contain bromelain. Bromelain is used as a meat tenderizer.

 S T E A M

Exploding Baggies

Explore how creating a chemical reaction can make a baggie pop!

by Chelsey Marashian **Buggy & Buddy**

Ingredients:

Zipper sandwich baggies
Square of toilet paper
Baking soda
White vinegar
Optional: food coloring or liquid watercolors
Measuring cup
Measuring spoons

Difficulty: ● ● ●

Estimated Project Time: 10 minutes

What's the STEAM behind it?

This activity is a great way to explore chemistry, specifically an acid-base reaction! Eventually the tissue full of baking soda in the baggie gets saturated with vinegar. The mixing of the baking soda (a base) and vinegar (an acid) create a chemical reaction, forming carbon dioxide gas. The gas fills the baggie and then runs out of room causing the explosion - POP!

Kids also get the opportunity to practice their math skills by measuring out the various ingredients for the experiment using measuring cups and measuring spoons.

   S T E A M

Instructions:

1. Find a spot to do this activity where you don't mind making a mess, like outside or your kitchen sink.

2. Pour ½ cup white vinegar into an empty zipper sandwich baggie.

3. Optional: Add some food coloring or liquid watercolor to your vinegar.

4. Place a square of toilet paper or a thin tissue down on the ground or nearby table.

5. Add approximately 1 ½ tablespoons of baking soda to the center of the tissue.

6. Fold the tissue up into a little packet, securing the baking soda inside.

7. Carefully and quickly drop the packet of baking soda into the baggie of vinegar and seal it shut completely.

8. Give it a little shake, set it down, move away, and watch what happens!

9. The baggie will begin to expand and eventually... POP!

10. If the baggie doesn't burst the first time, try adjusting the amount of vinegar and baking soda.

Project Extensions:

● Extend this project by altering some of the variables in the reaction.

  • Try varying the ratio of vinegar to baking soda. Can you find a ratio that works best?

  • Try out baggies of different sizes. Estimate how much vinegar and baking soda you will need to make the baggie burst.

  • Compare how long it takes the baggies to burst by using different packets to hold your baking soda: tissue, toilet paper, paper towel, etc.

● Incorporate art into this activity by using food coloring or liquid watercolors. Try adding two colors to your baggie of vinegar and see what the resulting color is. Or place two baggies with different colors next to each other and have them burst at the same time. Watch the colors mix as they seep out of the baggies!

● For more color chemistry, try to Make a Penny Turn Green.

Rock Candy

Learn about crystal formation with this candy creation project.

by P.R. Newton **STEAM Powered Family**

Difficulty: ● ● ● ● ●

Estimated Project Time: 90 minutes plus 3 days to grow crystals

What's the STEAM behind it?

Rock candy is produced from a supersaturated solution of sugar. A supersaturated solution simply means that the liquid has more solvent (sugar in this case) dissolved into it, than what could normally be achieved if dissolution took place under normal conditions (room temperature in this instance). The goal with rock candy is to create a 3:1 water to sugar solution.

To create a supersaturated solution the liquid needs to be hot while the sugar is added. Once the liquid starts to cool the sucrose crystals will form a solid crystalline structure. Hopefully on the stick creating our rock candy treat.

Ingredients:
4 x 2 cup mason jars
Candy sticks
4 clothes pins
4 quart saucepan
A metal spoon
Candy thermometer
6 cups of sugar plus ½ cup
for 'seeding' the sticks
2 cups of water
Food coloring
Flavoring if desired

 S T E A M

Instructions:

SAFETY NOTE: Adult supervision required as the hot sugar can cause serious burns.

1. Heat 2 cups of water and 1 cup of sugar. Simmer until liquid is clear. Add another cup of sugar, simmer until clear. Continue repeating until 6 cups of sugar are dissolved.

2. Gently boil until it reaches 110 Centigrade or 230 Fahrenheit, use a candy thermometer to carefully track the temperature. The mixture is now known as a supersaturated liquid.

3. Remove from heat. Take the lollipop sticks and dip into the syrup several times. Remember the syrup is very hot. Be careful. Now roll the wet stick in some sugar. Allow to dry. This step is 'seeding' the stick so that when you put it into the syrup the molecules will be attracted to the sugar and start crystallizing on the stick.

4. Into each mason jar add 6 drops of food coloring and flavoring if desired. Now carefully fill each jar approximately 2/3 full with the syrup.

5. Take the lollipop stick and lower the pointy end into the syrup. Make sure it doesn't touch the sides or the bottom of the jar. Use the clothes pin balanced across the neck of the jar to hold the stick in place.

6. It will take approximately 3 days for the crystals to form. Do not disturb the jars at all during this time. For best crystal formation keep the jars in a warm, dark place.

7. Remove from solution after 3 days and let dry on a paper towel before taste testing.

Project Extensions:

- Try different places for storing the jar. Do you get better crystal formation with warmer or cooler locations? Does light or dark affect the results?

- Love growing crystals? Here's the Secret To Super-Sized Crystals!

Cloud Soap

Explore the properties of soap with this fun experiment!

by Amber Scardino **Figment Creative Labs**

Difficulty: ●

Estimated Project Time: 10 minutes

What's the STEAM behind it?

Ivory soap contains air pockets that contain water molecules. When the Ivory soap is heated the water molecules evaporate and the heat causes the trapped air to expand. The heat softens the soap allowing the bar to expand as the air expands.

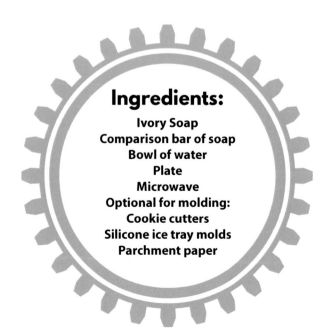

Ingredients:

Ivory Soap
Comparison bar of soap
Bowl of water
Plate
Microwave
Optional for molding:
Cookie cutters
Silicone ice tray molds
Parchment paper

Instructions:

1. First, explore the properties of the two bars of soap.

- Do a float test in the bowl of water to see which soap floats and which soap sinks.

- Try to break both soaps in half. If one doesn't break, an adult can cut it with a knife. Examine and compare the inside of soaps.

- Measure the soaps before and after heating. Compare.

2. Place Ivory soap on a microwavable plate and heat for 2 minutes on high. Watch the soap grow! Repeat with the other soap. Does it grow?

3. Take out and wait a minute before touching. The inside stays hot longer.

4. Bring the art in by creating shapes or sculptures with the softened soap.

Project Extensions:

● Explore other characteristics of soap with the Magic Milk Experiment on page 63.

Regrow Kitchen Scraps

Explore how plants grow with kitchen scraps.

by Anne Carey **Left Brain Craft Brain**

Difficulty:

Estimated Project Time: 10 minutes prep + several weeks growing time

What's the STEAM behind it?

When we use vegetables in the kitchen, the spare parts are often all that is needed to keep the plant growing. The roots, seeds, and leaves can turn into a new source of food.

Instructions:

1. For lettuce and celery regrowth, place root end in a small bowl or glass filled with just enough water to cover root. Once roots sprout, plant in soil.

2. For green onion regrowth, place root end in a small bowl or glass filled with just enough water to cover root. Chop off ends to use and continue to grow in water, changing it every few days.

3. For avocado regrowth, poke toothpicks into the pit and prop it up on top of a glass. Fill the glass with enough water to cover the bottom inch of the pit. When leaves appear, transplant to soil.

4. To regrow potatoes, cut out the eyes of a potato that have begun to sprout. Let dry overnight and then plant in soil.

5. To regrow pineapple, insert toothpicks into the leafy top and prop up on a glass. Once the roots grow, plant in soil.

Ingredients:
Vegetable kitchen scraps like:
Lettuce
Green onions
Celery
Sweet potatoes
Avocado pits
Pineapple tops
Water
Bowls or glasses
Toothpicks
Soil

Project Extensions:

- Try regrowing flowers. What part of a flower is needed to keep growing?

Growing Mold

Watch the wonder of fungus growth in this easy science experiment.

by Anne Carey **Left Brain Craft Brain**

Ingredients:

Petri dishes
2 1/2 tsp. sugar
2 1/2 tsp. agar powder
2 Cups beef broth
2 Cups water
Q-tips
Zipper bags
Bread or other food that molds

Difficulty: ● ● ● ●

Estimated Project Time: 4-5 days

What's the STEAM behind it?

Fungi are a group of organisms called eukaryotes that include single cell organisms like yeasts and mold. Multi-cell organisms like mushrooms are also a type of fungus. They have their own kingdom, along with plants, animals, protists and bacteria due their their unique cell structure. Fungi have five characteristics that separate them from the other kingdoms:

- Their cells contain nuclei like plants and animals.

- They can't photosynthesize like plants can.

- They absorb their food instead of making their own.

- Multi-cellular fungi grow via networks of long tubular filaments called hyphae.

- They usually reproduce via spores.

S T E A M

Instructions:

SAFETY NOTE: Wash your hands after handling fungus sample petri dishes and never touch the samples directly with your hands. A mask or other breathing protection is also recommended as breathing the spores can be dangerous.

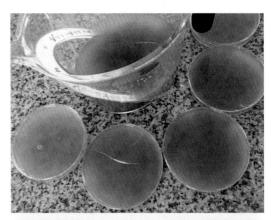

Make the Agar Plates

1. Pour the beef broth and water into a pan. Bring to a boil.

2. Add sugar and agar powder and stir over medium heat until dissolved.

3. Pour into petri dishes. Cool in refrigerator until hardened.

Test for Mold

1. Using a Q-tip, swipe across any surface that you want to test for mold. Then swipe Q-tip across a hardened agar plate. Be sure to use only one test area per petri dish.

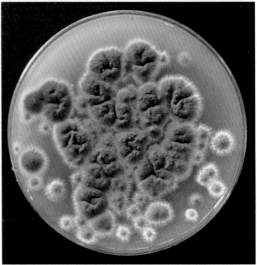

2. Cover petri dish and place inside a zipper bag. Store in a warm dark place until mold grows, approximately 4-5 days.

3. How many different types of fungus can you see on your samples?

Explore Food Mold

1. Grab your favorite food and let it sit in a zipper bag until fungus grows. Does it look the same as the samples you gathered with the Q-tips?

Make Fungus Art

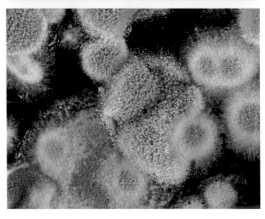

1. Once you know what color the fungus is, you can take a Q-tip sample and decorate your petri dish in a colorful pattern.

Project Extensions:

- As an extension to this fungi experiment, investigate the other five Kingdoms: Plants, Animals, Archaebacteria, Eubacteria, and Protists. Make a batch of Homemade Yogurt to learn about the beneficial bacteria in that delicious food.

EAT & DRINK

Pizza Bubbles

Did you know you can blow bubbles with cheese?

by Andra Weber **Andra Weber Creative**

Difficulty: ● ● ● ● ●
Estimated Project Time: 15 minutes
Makes 8 Servings with one container of cheese

Ingredients:
3 cups warm water
Medium-sized microwavable bowl
1 - 8 oz. container of fresh bocconcini mozzarella balls
Large spoon
Paper straws
Pizza dough
Pizza sauce

What's the STEAM behind it?

There is a lot of science behind cheese and what makes cheese stretch and melt. Cheese is made mostly of fat, protein and water. The casein protein is what gives structure to cheese and calcium is what glues the protein's structure together. Casein proteins trap fats and with the addition of more fat, a cheese is prone to better melting.

At about 90 degrees fahrenheit, milk fat begins to liquify and the cheese begins to soften. When cheese starts to warm, the bonds that hold the protein together begin to break and the cheese becomes softer. The calcium glue dissolves under the heat and the protein casein becomes stringy and tangled like rope. This creates a surface primed for stretching and perfect for making bubbles.

 S T E A M

Instructions:

SAFETY NOTE: Adult supervision required as the cheese will be hot.

1. Place 3 cups of warm water into a microwavable bowl. Put the bowl in the microwave for 1 minute and 30 seconds. Have an adult remove the bowl from the microwave. It will be hot.

2. Drop 1-2 mozzarella balls into the bowl. Let the cheese sit for 10 minutes.

3. After 10 minutes, use a spoon to gently scoop one mozzarella ball from the saucepan.

4. Ask an adult to test the cheese to make sure it is safe to handle. It should be soft and warm but not hot to the touch.

5. Working quickly, wrap a mozzarella ball around the end of a straw. Leave a gap between the cheese and the straw.

6. Gather the ends of the cheese around the straw's end. Grip the ends tight to create a seal.

7. Now puff slowly like blowing a balloon. Watch as the cheese stretches before your eyes!

8. Quickly remove the bubble from the straw and squeeze the ends to seal closed. Try another mozzarella ball if the first one pops.

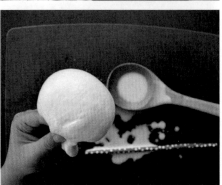

Make a Personal Pizza!
Form pizza dough into a small circle and top with pizza sauce. Place cheese bubble on top and bake according to package directions. Enjoy!

Project Extensions:

Try adding different cheeses to heated water. Do they soften? Why do you think some cheese melts faster than others? What happens to the mozzarella bubble when placed back into the warm water? Which cheeses have lots of milk fat? Do you think you can make bubbles from any other cheese? Why?

Layers of the Earth Pudding

Build a delicious model of the earth's core.

by Anne Carey **Left Brain Craft Brain**

Ingredients:

1 x 5.1 oz box instant vanilla pudding mix
1 x 3.9 oz box instant chocolate pudding mix
5 cups milk
Red, yellow, and green food coloring
1 cup shredded coconut
10 Oreos
1 cup mini marshmallows
8 x 5 oz. clear plastic cups
8 plastic dinosaur toys

Difficulty: ● ● ●

Estimated Project Time: 20 minutes + 1 1/2 hours chilling time

Makes 8 Servings

Project Extensions:

● Experiment with other ingredients to make another model of the earth. Could you do this with fruit or vegetables?

● This makes a great Earth Day project. Also be sure to check out these other Earth Day Science projects.

S T E A M

What's the STEAM behind it?

The earth is made up of multiple levels which vary in material and temperature. When volcanoes erupt, the molten liquid called lava is melted mantle and crust. Here are the layers of the earth:

Crust: This is the outer layer of the earth and is 0-60 km thick. The crust has two types, oceanic, which carries water, and continental, which carries land. The crust is solid, rocky and brittle and packed with calcium and sodium-aluminum silicates. The crust's temperature is about 0 ºC.

Mantle: The mantle is the next layer under the crust. It's the thickest layer of the Earth at nearly 2900 km. It's a semi-molten solid that can deform like a plastic. The top of the layer is hard like rock, but the bottom of the layer is melting due to temperature. The mantle's temperature is about 1000 ºC.

Outer Core: Traveling down into the Earth, you'll find the outer core. The outer core is a molten layer 2900-5100 km thick made up primarily of iron, sulfur and oxygen. The temperature here is about 3700 ºC. The outer core is the only liquid layer of the Earth.

Inner Core: The center of the Earth is the inner core and the hottest zone at ~5500 ºC. It's basically a big ball of solid iron about 5000-6000 km deep that floats in the middle of the outer core.

Pudding: The most delicious layer :)

Instructions:

1. Make chocolate and vanilla puddings in separate bowls according to the directions on the box.

2. Divide vanilla pudding into three small bowls and color one each in red, orange, and yellow. Mix well.

3. Chill all bowls of pudding for one hour. While pudding is chilling, prepare coconut and Oreo toppings.

4. Put shredded coconut in a zipper bag and add five drops of green food coloring. Close bag well and shake until coconut is green.

5. Put Oreos in a zipper bag, close bag well, and crush with a rolling pin.

6. Make the pudding cups by adding the layers to your plastic cup as follows. Each layer should completely cover the previous layer. Adjust amounts as necessary based upon your cup size and chill before serving.

   1. Inner Core: 6 mini marshmallows
   2. Inner Core: 1 tablespoon yellow vanilla pudding
   3. Outer Core: 1 tablespoon orange vanilla pudding
   4. Inner Mantle: 1 tablespoon red vanilla pudding
   5. Outer Mantle: 1 tablespoon chocolate pudding
   6. Crust: 1 tablespoon crushed Oreos
   7. Grass: 1 tablespoon green coconut
   8. 1 plastic dinosaur

Homemade Butter

Learn how to churn butter all in the name of science!

by Dayna Abraham **Lemon Lime Adventures**

Difficulty:

Estimated Project Time: 10 minutes

Makes 4 Servings

Ingredients:

Heavy whipping cream
Mason jar
Two small containers
Timer

What's the STEAM behind it?

Cream is what's called an emulsion, where one substance (fat) is suspended in another (water). The fat suspended in the water are groups of fat molecules surrounded by a membrane called globules.

When cream is shaken, the fat globules crash against each other, breaking the membrane. This lets the fat molecules out and they start separating from the liquid and clump together. Eventually, the fat molecules cling together in one giant clump forming butter. The liquid that remains is buttermilk!

   S T E A M

Instructions:

1. Start by pouring cream into a jar about 2/3 full and tightening the lid as tight as possible.

2. Now, shake! Shake, shake, shake (for about 5 minutes).

3. Use a timer to see how long it takes to start to see changes in the cream.

4. Once a ball is formed, stop shaking.

5. Seperate the "butter ball" from the left-over milk (buttermilk) and place into two small containers.

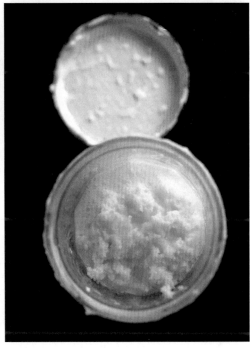

Project Extensions:

- Try shaking different kinds of creams to see if the butter forms differently and at a different rate. What happens if you use warm cream versus ice cold cream? Can you think of any other liquid that can be shaken to change it's properties?

- Do you like butter on your popcorn? Try this Popcorn Science experiment too!

Color Theory Candy

Learn about color theory and states of matter in this tasty project!

by Ana Dziengel **Babble Dabble Do**

Difficulty: ● ●

Estimated Project Time: 20 minutes + 30 minutes cooling time

Ingredients:
Red, blue, and yellow candy melts
Candy mold
Muffin tin
Craft sticks
Spoons

Note: Candy melts and molds are available at craft stores in the baking section

What's the STEAM behind it?

This project is a simple way to illustrate the basics of art color theory. The primary colors are red, blue, and yellow. Mixing two primary colors together makes the secondary colors: violet, green, and orange.

The different ratios of primary colors mixed will change the colors created. A ratio is a way of comparing values to one another. For example, using 2 parts yellow and 1 part blue will make a different color than using 1 part yellow and 2 parts blue. Use measuring spoons to keep track of the different color ratios in the colors.

This project also explores "states of matter." The three most commonly known states of matter are solids, liquids, and gases. Materials can change from one state to another when heated or cooled. Adding heat to the candy melts it into a semi-liquid state for mixing. Quickly cooling it turns it back into a solid.

 S T E A M

Instructions:

Tip: This is messy! Cover work surface with butcher paper before starting.

1. (Adults only) Melt the candy in the microwave or on the stove in a double boiler following the directions on the bag.

2. Place the melted candy next to the muffin tin and candy molds. Add a spoonful of two primary colors to one of the muffin cups and stir using a craft stick to create a secondary color.

3. When the color is mixed, spread some melted candy in the candy mold using a craft stick.

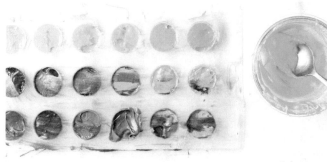

4. Repeat to make different colors. Don't forget to make a few candies from the primary colors!

5. When the candy mold is filled, take a craft stick and scrape the excess candy off the top of the mold.

6. Place in the refrigerator to cool for about 15-30 minutes.

7. Once cooled, pop them out, compare colors, and enjoy!

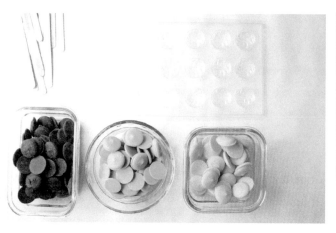

Project Extensions:

- Try mixing in white candy melts to form different values of colors. A value is the lightness or darkness of a color.

- How many different colors can be made? Experiment with different ratios of primary colors to make as many different colors as possible. Document the ratios in a chart.

- Explore color mixing some more with these <u>Dip-Dyed Craft Sticks</u> or learn about centrifugal force with <u>Color Spin Mixing.</u>

Edible Frog Life Cycle

Learn about life science in the kitchen with these edible amphibians.

by Karyn Tripp **Teach Beside Me**

Ingredients:

Plain gelatin
Non-stick spray
Lemon juice
**Honey or other natural
sweetener**
Green grapes
Small spinach leaves
Green apple
Raisins
Shredded carrots
Toothpicks
Semi-sphere mold

Difficulty: ● ●

Estimated Project Time: 10 minutes plus several hours chilling time

Makes 1 Serving

What's the STEAM behind it?

Frogs go through 3 distinct phases before they become adults: egg, tadpole, and froglets. A frog is laid as an **egg** by its mother. Once it hatches, it is a **tadpole** and is equipped with a tail and external gills like a fish. Next the tadpole transforms into a **froglet** and grows legs. Finally, the froglet will retract its tail and become an adult **frog**.

This transformation is metamorphosis which is the process that creatures go through to transform to mature adults.

S T E A M

Instructions:

SAFETY NOTE: Toothpicks should be removed before eating.

Frog Eggs:

1. Make a pack of plain gelatin following the package directions using lemon juice for the liquid and honey for the sweetener.

2. Grease molds with non-stick spray and pour gelatin into molds.

3. Place in refrigerator for about an hour of chilling, then add the raisins.

4. Let them chill a few more hours until solid.

5. Carefully remove the "eggs" from the molds. It works best to run around the edge with a knife first.

Tadpoles:

1. Grab several green grapes and small baby spinach leaves.

2. Poke the stem of the spinach into the end of the grape. If it does not go in easily, use a toothpick to make the hole bigger.

Froglets:

1. Use another grape and add shredded carrots for legs and another spinach leaf for the tail of the froglet. Poke the holes for the legs with toothpicks first to make it easier to put the carrot pieces in.

Frog:

1. Cut a sliver out of the apple for the mouth.

2. Attach the raisins as eyes with toothpicks broken in half.

3. Cut grapes in half and use as legs. Attach with toothpicks.

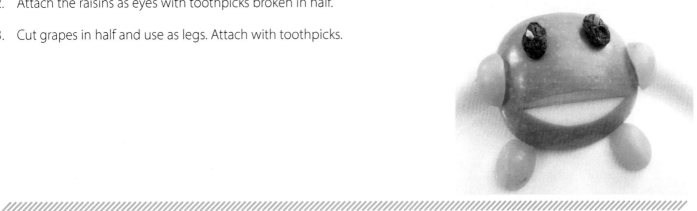

Project Extensions:

- Talk about the life cycles of other animals like chickens and fish. How do they compare to frogs?

Unicorn Noodles

Use science to make these magical noodles change color!

by Anne Carey **Left Brain Craft Brain**

Difficulty: ● ● ● ●
Estimated Project Time: 30 minutes
Makes 4 Servings

Ingredients:

1 package rice noodles
1/2 purple cabbage
5 slices cucumber
1/2 cup pomegranate seeds
1 lemon, cut into wedges
Salt and pepper, to taste
Butter or soy sauce, for serving

What's the STEAM behind it?

Science gives these magical color-changing unicorn noodles their gorgeous hues. The rice noodles are soaked in boiled cabbage water. Why? Cabbage juice acts as an indicator, meaning it changes color as the pH changes. A magical water-soluble pigment in red cabbage called anthocyanin changes color when it is mixed with an acid or a base. It's purple when in contact with neutral pH liquids (think water), pink when it touches acids (think lemon juice) and green when it touches bases (think baking soda).

Instructions:

1. Place the cabbage in a large stockpot and cover with water.

2. Boil until the water is deeply saturated with purple color and remove from heat, approximately 10 minutes.

3. Remove the cabbage and discard. Place the rice noodles in the purple water. Let them soak for 7-8 minutes until soft, then remove half, and let the remaining half soak for an additional 5 minutes.

4. While the noodles are soaking, cut the cucumber into shapes for garnish.

5. Drain the cabbage water (save it for another experiment!) and swirl together the blue and purple noodles. The longer the noodles soak, the deeper the colors will be.

6. Serve with a sprinkle of pomegranate seeds, salt, pepper and cute cucumber shape accents. Place the lemons on the side for a magic transformation.

7. Have the kids squeeze a bit of lemon onto their noodles and watch as the noodles slowly change to pink! (Alternatively, soak a few of the noodles in lemon juice to have some pink ones to swirl in. Just be sure to rinse them before serving for the best taste.)

8. Adjust with butter or soy sauce to taste.

Project Extensions:

 Make your own pH paper with the leftover cabbage juice. Dip some coffee filters into the cabbage juice until soaked and hang up to dry. Cut the filters into pieces and use them to test various household materials. If it's purple, it's neutral; if it's pink, it's acidic; and if it's green, it's basic.

    S T E A M

Crystal Cupcakes

Make beautiful cupcake toppers that reflect the sun's rays.

by Andra Weber **Andra Weber Creative**

Ingredients:

12 frosted cupcakes
1 lb of clear hard candies in various colors
12 aluminum foil squares measured and cut 3.5" x 3.5"
1 wooden spoon
Seal-tight sandwich bags (1 bag per candy color)
Safety goggles
1 baking sheet

Difficulty: ● ● ● ● ●

Estimated Project Time: 30 minutes + cooling time

Makes 12 Cupcakes

S T E A M

What's the STEAM behind it?

Making candy suncatchers is where art and science come together. This candy is made of sugar which is a crystal compound that is naturally found in most plants. Mass produced sugar usually comes from either sugarcane or sugar beets due to their high sugar content.

Sugar is a compound called carbohydrate and is made up of carbon, hydrogen, and oxygem. A compound is a substance formed when two or more elements are chemically joined.

When candy is in it's "hard crack" or solid state the molecules are packed so tight they can't move around. These tightly packed molecules make candy a solid. However, with the oven's heat, the molecules have space to move and the solid becomes a liquid at the temperature called the melting point. When the candy then cools, it returns to it's original solid state. It, however, is in a new form where the colors have adhered together, creating the design of the suncatcher. When the cooled candy is placed into sunlight, a design appears as the sun travels through the transparent candy..

Instructions:

SAFETY NOTE: Adult supervision required as the hot sugar can cause serious burns.

1. Preheat oven to 350 degrees.

2. Unwrap and sort candies by color.

3. Place candies into seal-tight bags, one candy color per bag. On a hard work surface, with safety goggles on, use the wooden spoon to smash candies into small pieces.

4. Place squares of aluminum foil onto a baking sheet and form circle shapes with the foil.

5. Sprinkle one candy color onto the aluminum foil and push the candy to the sides of the foil.

6. Repeat with more colors until the bottom of each foil piece is covered.

7. Have an adult bake it in the oven for 3-5 minutes until the candy is melted.

8. Let cool for 30 minutes. An adult should test the candy to insure it's 100% cool before removing the aluminum foil.

9. Insert one candy suncatcher on each cupcake.

10. Just before eating, display the cupcakes in the sun. Watch the designs sparkle and reflect their designs in the sun's rays.

Project Extensions:

Before placing the candy into the aluminum foil, sketch out some designs. How do the designs translate in the melted candy? What happens when the candy suncatcher is placed in different light sources? What happens to the design? Which light works best at reflecting the design? Do you think all candy would melt with heat? Why?

Green Eggs

Green eggs and ham can be more than a fun children's story!

by Karyn Tripp **Teach Beside Me**

Difficulty: ●●●

Estimated Project Time: 20 minutes

What's the STEAM behind it?

The juice from red cabbage is a natural pH indicator. It changes colors when it comes in contact with an acid or base. The egg whites are a base which creates a reaction turning it green. .

Makes 1 Serving

Ingredients:

Red cabbage water (see the instructions in the Cabbage Juice Science experiment on page 62)
2 Eggs
2 small bowls
Frying pan
Butter or cooking spray

Instructions:

1. Separate the yolks from the whites of the eggs into separate bowls.

2. Add 1-2 tablespoons red cabbage liquid to the whites and whisk until blended.

3. Grease a small frying pan with butter or cooking spray and heat it to medium high heat.

4. Pour the egg whites into the frying pan and cook for one minute. The whites will turn green and will brighten as they cook.

5. Add the yolk back on top to cook with the white. Cook for another minute.

6. Gently flip the eggs to cook until set to the desired doneness.

Project Extensions:

● Test some other foods you eat to see if they react in similar ways. Are your favorite foods acidic or basic?

● Does ham turn green too?

    S T E A M

Raindrop Cake

Learn what makes a raindrop round and eat some water cake!

by Anne Carey **Left Brain Craft Brain**

Difficulty: ● ● ●

Estimated Project Time: 15 minutes + 1 hour chilling time

Makes 4 Servings

What's the STEAM behind it?

What makes a raindrop round? It's a phenomenon called surface tension which makes the surface of a liquid that is in contact with gas act like a thin elastic sheet. It's like a skin holding all the water in the drop together.

This Japanese cake called Mizu Shingen Mochi uses agar, a vegan gelatin, to form the spherical shape instead of surface tension.

Instructions:

1. Boil water in a medium saucepan.

2. Add agar powder. Stir until dissolved.

3. Add sugar. Stir until dissolved.

4. Remove from heat and pour into sphere mold. Chill until firm, about 1 hour.

5. Serve with honey, maple syrup, or molasses.

6. Optional: mix in cut up fruit or sprinkles after pouring into mold for flavor variations or to make designs in the raindrop cake.

Ingredients:

2 cups spring water (spring water will taste better than tap water)
1/2 teaspoon agar powder
1/2 teaspoon sugar
2 sphere or half sphere molds

Toppings like honey, maple syrup, molasses
Mix-ins like fruit, sprinkles

Project Extensions:

● Observe drops of water on a smooth surface with a magnifying glass. Dip a toothpick into dishwasher soap and then into the water drop. How did it change shape?

Funny Muffins

Bake muffins without eggs? How funny!

by Andra Weber **Andra Weber Creative**

Difficulty: ●●●●●
Estimated Project Time: 40 minutes
Makes 12 Muffins

Ingredients:

1-1/2 cups all purpose flour
1 cup granulated sugar
¼ cup cocoa
1/2 teaspoon salt
1 cup cold water
1/3 cup vegetable oil
1 teaspoon vanilla
1 teaspoon baking soda
1 teaspoon white vinegar
2/3 cup chocolate chips
Paper cupcake liners

What's the STEAM behind it?

Baking is edible science!

Eggs can be used as a leavening agent, provide moisture, or act as a binder in recipes. In the case of muffins, eggs give the muffin shape and add structure by combining with the flour proteins and flour starches. Heat from the oven sets the proteins and starches around tiny air bubbles which creates the structure for muffins.

When eggs are replaced with baking soda and an acid such as vinegar, a chemical reaction takes place. This chemical reaction produces tiny carbon dioxide bubbles that provide the muffin's structure and the bubbles combined with heat, help give muffins their shape.

S T E A M

Instructions:

1. Preheat the oven to 350 degrees.

2. Line a muffin tin with 12 cupcake liners.

3. Place flour, sugar, cocoa, and salt in a medium bowl and mix.

4. Mix the water, oil, and vanilla in a large bowl. Then add the flour mixture and combine until smooth.

5. In the center of the batter add the baking soda and pour the 1 tablespoon vinegar on top of the baking soda.

6. Mix together until smooth and add the chocolate chips.

7. With an ice cream scoop, place the batter into the 12 muffin cups.

8. Ask an adult to slide the muffin tin into the oven and bake for 22-25 min or until a toothpick comes out clean.

9. Ask an adult to remove the muffin tin from the oven and let cool.

Project Extensions:

- Do the eggless muffins look, taste or smell funny? What are other leavening agents? Could they be used to give muffins their shape? Could lemon juice be used in place of vinegar? Why? What other baked goods could be made without eggs?

Ice Cream Lab

Who knew how much science goes into a an ice cream sundae?

by Anne Carey **Left Brain Craft Brain**

Difficulty: ● ● ●

Estimated Project Time: 30 minutes

Makes 2 Servings

What's the STEAM behind it?

How does shaking the ingredients make ice cream?
Ice cream is an emulsion, which means small droplets of one liquid disperse or spread throughout another liquid. In ice cream, particles of liquid fat are dispersed throughout the water from the half & half, sugar, and ice.

What makes ice cream creamy? Ice cream is made of sugar, fat, ice crystals and air. The more you shake, the smaller the ice crystals become and the more air is incorporated into the ice cream and the creamier it gets.

Why does the magic shell topping get crispy? It's because it's made with coconut oil, which is a solid at room temperature. Warming it up and then pouring over cold ice cream makes the topping go from liquid to solid.

Ingredients:

For the Ice Cream:
1 cup half and half
½ teaspoon vanilla
2 tablespoons sugar
1 quart sized zipper plastic bag
1 gallon sized zipper plastic bag
Ice
Salt
Dish towel

For the Magic Shell:
2 cups chocolate chips
1/4 cup refined coconut oil

Ice cream toppings: crushed Oreos, sprinkles, chocolate chips, etc.

S T E A M

Instructions:

Make the Ice Cream:

1. Pour 1 cup half and half, 2 tablespoons sugar, and ½ teaspoon vanilla extract into a quart sized zipper bag. Close tightly.

2. Fill the gallon sized zipper bag full with ice and sprinkle generously with salt.

3. Place small bag inside the ice bag and close tightly.

4. Wrap bag with a dish towel and start shaking! Ice cream will be ready after about 10-15 minutes of shaking.

Make the Magic Shell:

1. Place chocolate chips and coconut oil into a microwave-safe bowl and heat on high for 30 second intervals. Stir in between each interval. Continue heating until melted. Do not overcook.

Build A Sundae:

1. Scoop ice cream into a dish, top with warm magic shell, and toppings. Wait a minute for the magic shell to harden and dig in!

Project Extensions:

- Why do you add salt to the ice? Extend this project by doing the ice building project on page 22.

- What other flavors of ice cream and Magic Shell can you make? How would you change the recipes?

Pendulum Cookies

Build a pendulum to design and decorate cookies.

by Andra Weber **Andra Weber Creative**

Ingredients:

For the Pendulum:
2 large unopened cereal boxes, approximately 13" or taller
1.5 ft of string
Metal ruler or wooden spoon, at least 1 foot long
Masking tape
Parchment paper

1 batch sugar cookies, baked and cooled

For the Icing
1 plastic sealable sandwich bag
1 cup confectioners sugar
1 teaspoon vanilla extract
Food coloring of choice
2 tablespoons milk

Difficulty: ● ● ● ●

Estimated Project Time: 20 minutes

Makes 24 cookies

What's the STEAM behind it?

The bag of icing suspended from the cereal boxes creates a pendulum or weight suspended from a pivot. Because the icing can swing freely, when the bag is moved sideways from its resting position, it is subject to a force due to gravity that will move it back toward its resting position. The oscillations, or movement back and forth at a regular speed, create specific designs that are proportional yet abstract.

 S T E A M

Instructions:

Set Up the Work Area: Place a rectangle of parchment paper on a work space and arrange 9-12 cookies on the paper.

Make the Frosting: Measure 1 cup sugar, and place in a small bowl. Add 1-2 tablespoons milk, vanilla, and food coloring to the bowl and mix. (The icing should be very runny.)

Build the Pendulum:

1. Tape the ends of the ruler or wooden spoon to the top of the cereal boxes. Then put the boxes with ruler or spoon on top of the paper, straddling the cookies.

2. Fill the sandwich bag with icing and seal closed. Twist the bag into a cone shape. Tie the string to the bag's top.

3. Loop, tighten, and tie the other end of the string over the ruler or spoon. The bag should hover about 3" above the cookies.

4. Cut a very small hole in the tip of the bag and swing the bag sideways and watch the pendulum oscillate around and decorate the cookies.

5. Once the first color is done, remove, attach and repeat icing directions if other colors are desired.

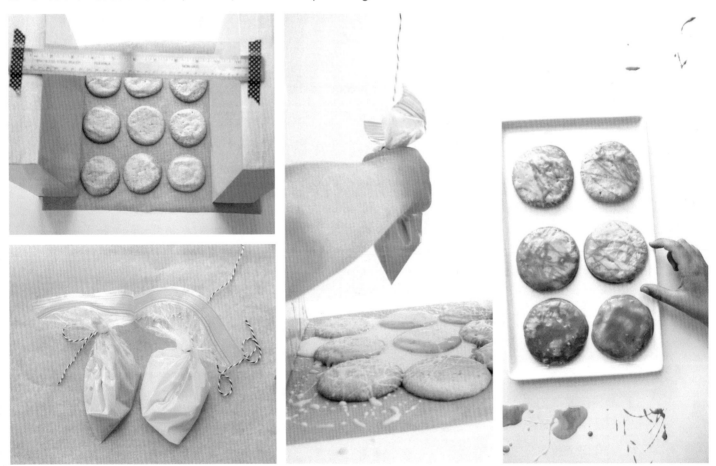

Project Extensions:

- Try hanging the icing bag from a taller box and a longer string. How is the design different? Does the design change when you swing the icing bag faster? Slower? What happens to the proportion of the design with the changes to the mechanics?

S T E A M

Rock Chocolate

Explore how rocks are formed with something tastier than stones!

Difficulty: ● ● ●

Estimated Project Time: 30 minutes

Makes 2 servings.

What's the STEAM behind it?

There are three main types of rocks on Earth:

Sedimentary rocks are made up of small pieces of other rocks that have been compressed together. Examples are limestone and sandstone.

Metamorphic rocks are rocks that have been transformed by heat, pressure, and chemical reactions. This often happens deep under the Earth's surface. Examples are slate and marble.

Igneous rocks are made up of cooled magma. Examples are basalt and granite.

Ingredients:

White and milk chocolate bars
Grater or vegetable peeler
Cutting board
Aluminum foil
Cookie sheet

by Anne Carey **Left Brain Craft Brain**

Instructions:

1. Grate white and milk chocolate into a small bowl.

For Sedimentary Rocks:

1. Sprinkle some chocolate shavings into a piece of aluminum foil and press with a spoon until compressed together.

For Metamorphic Rocks:

1. Wrap up the sedimentary chocolate rock completely in foil.

2. Press foil between your hands for several minutes to warm up the chocolate and squish it together.

For Igneous Rocks:

1. Preheat oven to 350 degrees.

2. Form a square of aluminum foil into a rock shaped mold and sprinkle chocolate into mold.

3. Place molds on cookie sheet and have an adult place in oven until melted, about 5 minutes. Let cool.

Project Extensions:

● Check out the lava toffee on the next page which is a perfect example of igneous (candy) rock!

S T E A M

Lava Toffee

Love a good eruption? Here is a candy version that tastes amazing!

by P.R. Newton **STEAM Powered Family**

Difficulty: ● ● ●
Estimated Project Time: 2 hours including cooling
Makes 12 servings.

What's the STEAM behind it?

Lava toffee has a chemical reaction similar to baking soda and vinegar, but instead of an acid heat starts the reaction with baking soda. CO_2 gas is released which is what causes the eruption. As sugars cool they keep the bubbly formation.

Instructions:

1. Grease the disposable tin pan with butter.

2. In a large saucepan heat the sugar and syrup over a medium-low temperature. Stir until it starts to bubble and then leave it with the candy thermometer in until it reaches 150C (300F). Don't remove it early or the toffee will stick to your teeth like cement!

3. Remove from the heat.

4. Stir in the bicarbonate soda and watch it bubble up. The kids can help add the bicarbonate soda, but have an adult do the stirring. Don't get the kids too close as the reaction takes place. Splashing may happen.

5. Once it is mixed and the reaction is going, pour the toffee into the prepared pan and leave for 1 ½ hours to cool before breaking or cutting up into pieces.

Ingredients:
**1 cup of sugar
½ cup of golden syrup
(i.e. syrup, honey,
or molasses)
2 teaspoons of bicarbonate
of soda (aka baking soda)
Candy thermometer
(this is very important as
temperature is critical)
Disposable tin pan
Butter**

Project Extensions:

● For an added flavor experience, try adding chocolate! What do you need to do to make it set up smoothly?

● Love experimenting with chemistry? Try these other Candy Science Activities.

Bread in a Bag

Learn about microrganisms and fermentation in this crusty, delicious bread.

by Anne Carey **Left Brain Craft Brain**

Difficulty:

Estimated Project Time: 30 minutes prep time + 40 minute rise time + 35 minute bake time

Makes 2 loaves

Ingredients:

1 large freezer zipper bag
3 cups flour, separated
1 0.25 oz. packet rapid rise yeast
1 cup warm water
3 Tablespoons white sugar
3 Tablespoons olive oil
1 1/2 teaspoon salt
Butter or non-stick spray for greasing pans
2 loaf pans

Project Extensions:

Observe the yeast in action! Grab an extra bag of yeast and pour it into a measuring cup filled with 1 cup warm water and 32 tablespoons sugar. Note the volume of the contents. Mix and watch the yeast rise for ten minutes. How much did the volume change?

Try making what's called an unleavened bread, a bread that does not have yeast or another ingredient that makes it rise such as baking powder or buttermilk. Examples of unleavened bread are tortillas, pita, and even crepes!

  E
S T E A M

What's the STEAM behind it?

Bread owes its delicious, spongy self to yeast and flour. Here's how it works:

What is yeast? Yeasts are single cell microorganisms in the Fungi kingdom. Yeasts are important in the world of baking, alcohol production and even the pharmaceutical industry as they help scientists create new medicines. Yeasts survive by eating carbohydrates like fructose or glucose and use their enzymes to break the sugars down into usable components. This sugar breakdown is called fermentation and converts carbohydrates to carbon dioxide (CO_2) and alcohols.

What makes bread dough rise? The CO_2 given off by the yeast creates bubbles in the bread dough and causes the bread to rise. When it goes into the oven, the heat causes the CO_2 to expand even more and the bread to get taller.

What is gluten and why is it in bread? If the bread didn't have a strong, elastic network to contain the CO_2, the bubbles would pop, just like chewing gum. Luckily, wheat flour has an elastic network called gluten. The more gluten, the stronger the gas bubbles will be and the more the dough will rise. As the bread bakes, the gluten hardens and the air pockets stay, creating that fluffy, airy, soft texture we love in bread.

Instructions:

1. In a large resealable zipper bag, add 1 cup of flour, 3 tablespoons of white sugar, 1 packet of yeast and 1 cup of warm water. Press as much air out of the bag as possible and close tightly. Now mix and squish the bag with your hands until the dough is uniformly mixed. Set aside to rest for 10 minutes at room temperature, or until the CO_2 bubbles appear and the bag inflates.

2. In a small bowl, stir together 1 cup of flour, olive oil and salt. Pour into the bag and again press out as much air as possible. Close and squish until well mixed.

3. Add the last cup of flour to the bag, and mix until the dough is uniformly mixed and no flour pockets exist.

4. Remove the dough from the bag and place on a lightly floured surface. Knead for 8 to 10 minutes. Form into two small loaves, and place each into a greased 8"x4" inch loaf pan. Cover with towels, and let to rise for about 30 minutes, or until your finger leaves an impression when you poke the top of the loaf. Colder areas may require longer rise times.

5. Preheat the oven to 375 degrees F.

6. Bake the bread for 35 minutes in the preheated oven, until golden brown.

Drinkable Lava Lamp

Molecular gastronomy makes this drink fun!

by Amber Scardino **Figment Creative Labs**

Ingredients:

1/2 teaspoon agar
2/3 cup + 3 teaspoons juice of choice
Vegetable oil
Large bottle of sparkling water

Tools:

Whisk
Small sauce pan
A tall glass
Syringe or dropper
Candy thermometer
Sieve /strainer
Bowl
Funnel

Difficulty:

Estimated Project Time: 20 minutes + 30 minutes freezing time

Makes 2 Servings

What's the STEAM behind it?

Use the molecular gastronomy technique called gelification to make juice balls. Pop them into your glass to turn them into a fizzy lava lamp drink. The juicy drops in the lava lamp use a gelling agent called agar. Agar is one of many different hydrocolloids, a substance that creates a gel in the presence of water. The spheres float throughout the lava lamp with the help of carbonated sparkling water.

Instructions:

1. Chill a tall glass of oil in the freezer for 30 minutes.

2. Pour 2/3 cup of juice into a saucepan.

3. Add agar and keep whisking while heating on medium heat until it comes to a boil.

4. Remove juice / agar mixture from heat. Put candy thermometer in and wait for it to come to around 120-130 deg. F (50-53 deg. C)

5. Take cup of oil out of the freezer.

6. Use the dropper to drop drops of the liquid into the cold oil. Hold syringe a few inches above the cup, so the drops have enough force to travel through the oil.

7. Pour the oil out, using a sieve to strain the spheres and rinse the spheres well with water to get all of the oil off.

8. Taste the spheres!

9. Pour a small amount of bubbly water out of the bottle into a cup to create more space in the bottle (You can always pour some back in after you fill the bottle with the spheres.)

10. Use the funnel to pour the spheres into the water bottle.

11. Put the top back on the bottle and play with the lava lamp.

12. Feel free to drink. The sooner the better. The spheres lose color over time.

Project Extensions:

- You could eat these flavorful spheres alone or add them to any dessert. Try them in the Ice Cream Lab on page 112.

- Instead of making spheres, try different gelling techniques to make cubes, noodles, sheets, and become a molecular gastronomist! Pouring the gelling liquid into straws will make worms!

   S T E A M

Homemade Orange Soda

Don't buy soda, make it, with a simple chemical reaction!

by Leslie Manlapig **Pink Stripey Socks**

Difficulty: ●

Estimated Project Time: 5 minutes

What's the STEAM behind it?

Orange juice is an acid and baking soda is a base. When mixed together, they react, releasing carbon dioxide. That's what makes the orange juice taste slightly fizzy, like soda. Soda's fizziness is also due to carbon dioxide. However, instead of relying on an acid-base reaction, soda manufacturers create that distinctive bubbly sensation by forcing carbon dioxide into liquids at very high pressures.

Ingredients:

**Glass
Orange juice
Baking soda**

Instructions:

1. Pour 1/2 C of juice into your glass.

2. Add in 1/8 tsp of baking soda.

3. Mix the two together and sip!

Project Extensions:

● Try mixing the baking soda with other liquids (like tea, milk, water, or other types of juice) to see if you get the same fizzy sensation. Make predictions and then test them! Why do you think some combinations resulted in fizzy drinks and others did not?

● Try this Magic Fizzy Sand for more fun with acid-base reactions.

    S T E A M

Sweet Slushy Science

Make a homemade slushy and learn about reactions!

by P.R. Newton **STEAM Powered Family**

Difficulty: ●

Estimated Project Time: 2-3 hours

What's the STEAM behind it?

In this experiment, the principles of heat transfer and the effect of salt on ice make for a frozen treat. The salt sprinkled on the ice causes an endothermic reaction that pulls heat from around it to melt the ice. It does this so aggressively that it will drop the temperature around it below freezing which allows the juice to freeze.

Instructions:

1. Pour juice into a plastic cup.

2. Place cup in the center of the large bowl. Add ice to the bowl until at least 3/4 of the juice cup is covered with ice.

3. Carefully sprinkle a large amount of salt on the ice, making sure not to spill any into the juice.

4. Now wait... This takes a few hours.

5. Stir the juice every 30 minutes until slushee reaches desired consistency. Do not skip this step or you will have a juice cube instead of a slushy!

Ingredients:

Small plastic cup
Large bowl
Ice (lots!)
Course rock salt
Juice
Spoon or stir stick
Slurpee straws
Non-contact infrared thermometer (optional)

Project Extensions:

● While waiting, periodically measure the temperature of the slushy with a non-contact infrared thermometer and record readings on a table.

S T E A M

Edible Water Bubbles

Drink your water in bubble form with this molecular gastronomy project!

by Anne Carey **Left Brain Craft Brain**

Difficulty: ● ● ● ● ●
Estimated Project Time: 45 minutes
Makes 4 Servings

Ingredients:

**1 gram or 1/2 teaspoon
sodium alginate
5 grams or 1 1/2 teaspoons
calcium lactate
Water
1 small bowl
2 large bowls
Scale
Immersion blender
Food coloring (optional)
Tablespoon measuring spoon**

What's the STEAM behind it?

These edible water bubbles owe their form to reverse spherification, a process used in molecular gastronomy. Spherification was discovered by mistake by a food scientist in the 1940's. It's simply the method of turning a food item into the shape of a sphere.

This process works because calcium ions in the calcium lactate solution cause the sodium alginate to gel. But only the surface alginate gels, creating a thin film with liquid inside.

  S T E A M

Instructions:

1. Blend 1 gram sodium alginate in 1 cup of water in a small bowl with an immersion blender. Set aside for 10-15 minutes until there are no air bubbles and solution is crystal clear.

2. While sodium alginate solution is resting, mix 5 grams calcium lactate in 4 cups of water with a spoon or spatula until completely dissolved. Add food coloring if desired.

3. Scoop a tablespoon full of the sodium alginate solution and gently lower into the calcium lactate bath. Tip the spoon slowly so the bubble won't break.

4. Gently stir the calcium lactate bath for 2-3 minutes until bubbles have a jelly-like surface and don't break when touched.

5. Fill a bowl with water about two thirds full. Gently remove bubbles from calcium lactate bath and place into the water bowl to rinse.

6. Remove and eat! Or is it drink?

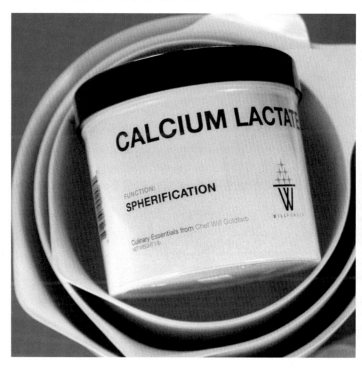

Project Extensions:

- Try this recipe with juice too!! The bubbles are delicious. Juices without added citric or ascorbic acid work best due to their pH.

- Make edible smoothie bubbles too! Pick a yogurt with full fat and at least 20% of the daily recommended calcium % in the nurtition ingredients. Carefully drop tablespoonfuls into the sodium alginate made for the water bubbles and stir for several minutes.

Color Changing Lemonade

Learn about pH with this delicious lemonade.

by Anne Carey **Left Brain Craft Brain**

Difficulty: ● ● ● ● ●
Estimated Project Time: 10 minutes
Makes 4 Servings

Ingredients:

Butterfly pea flower tea bag
1 cup water
4 cups lemonade
1 lemon (optional)

What's the STEAM behind it?

There's a very special ingredient in this lemonade. Butterfly pea flowers. Butterfly pea flowers contain a vivid blue pigment called anthocyanin. Anthocyanin has a unique capability to act as an indicator, meaning it changes color as the pH changes. It appears bright blue at high (basic) pH's and transitions to a vivid pink at low (acidic) pH's. This is why you can turn your lemonade from yellow to purple to pink as you stir your butterfly tea into the drink. The flowers and tea are a common ingredient in countries like Thailand where they like to serve the tea with honey and lemon.

S T E A M

Instructions:

1. With adult supervision, heat water to near boiling, add tea bag and let steep for 3-4 minutes or until tea is a deep blue color. Chill.

2. Fill four glasses with ice. Add one cup of lemonade to each glass.

3. Serve with a small shot glass or beaker filled with 1/4 cup butterfly pea flower tea and a straw for stirring.

4. Add the tea and watch the color change!

5. Want an even more pink drink? Squeeze some lemon juice into the glass.

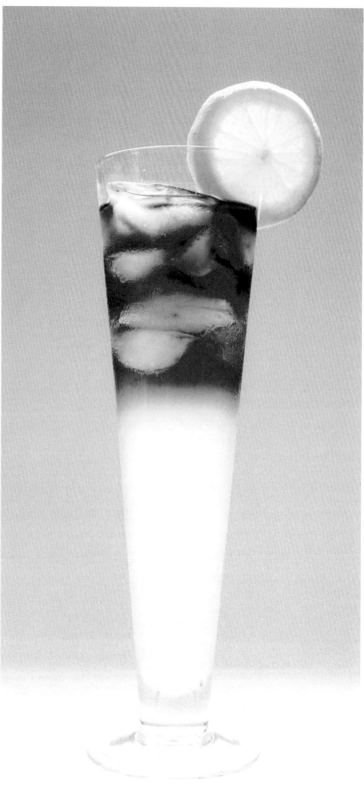

Project Extensions:

- For an added challenge, make a pH scale with the butterfly flower tea. You'll need something with plastic wells like a paint palette or plastic egg carton as well as a pipette.

  1. Steep 1 bag of tea in 1 cup boiling water for 4 minutes.

  2. Place 10 drops of tea in each well.

  3. Add lemon juice in increasing number of drops in each well. For example, 1 drop in first well, 2 drops in second well, 3 drops in third well, etc.

  4. Note how the color changes.

- Try making Color Changing Slime to learn about temperature driven color changes called thermochromism.

APPENDIX

STEAM EXTENSION PROJECTS

Like what you found in STEAM Kids in the Kitchen?
Check out these extension projects that keep curious minds growing.

These are the extensions projects mentioned at the bottom of the projects in the rest of the book.

For easy clickthrough links, go to:

steamkidsbooks.com/kitchen-extensions.

- Pop-Up Light-Up Paper Flower Card
- Backyard Pulley
- Hands-Free Ice Cube Boat Race
- Maple Syrup Candy!
- Robot Playdough with Deconstructed Computer Parts
- Sinking Soda Surprise
- DIY Conveyor Belt
- Tin Can Toy Car
- Spinning Top Marker Art
- Weather Jar
- Recycled Suspension Bridge
- Mystery Bag Challenges
- Rainbow Reactions
- Bottle Rockets
- Bubble Painting
- Bubble Lava Lamp
- Tchuka Ruma Game
- Dara Game
- Secret Message Valentines
- Leaf and Flower Pounding

- Sink or Float Experiment
- Stained Glass Pasta
- Homemade Salt Dough.
- Magic Milk Designs on Paper
- Candy Chromatography Experiment.
- Water Drop Races
- Homemade Watercolor Sparkle Paint
- String Art Geometry
- 3-D Geometric Shapes
- Precise Gelatin Prints Using Stencils
- Make a Penny Turn Green
- Secret To Super-Sized Crystals
- Homemade Yogurt
- Earth Day Science projects.
- Popcorn Science
- Dip-Dyed Craft Sticks
- Color Spin Mixing
- Candy Science Activities
- Magic Fizzy Sand
- Color Changing Slime

Um el Tuweisat Gameboard

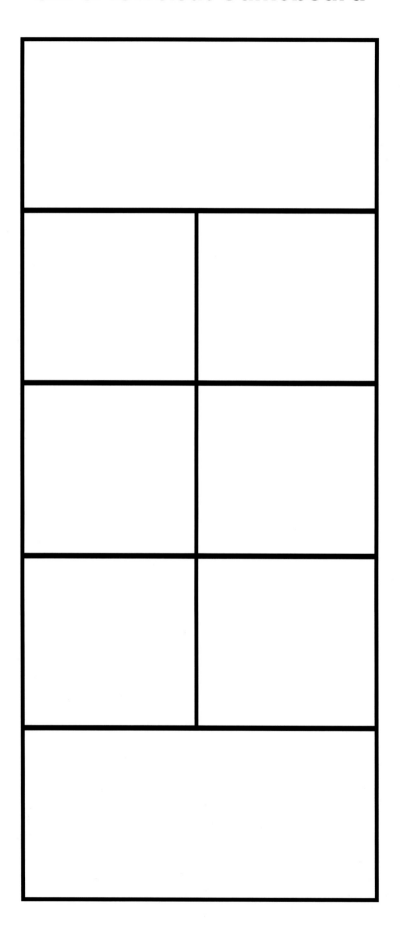

INDEX

STEAM INDEX

ENGINEERING (CONT'D)

ART

ART (CONT'D)

MATH

INDEX

Meet the Authors

Anne Carey
Left Brain Craft Brain

Anne is an MIT-educated chemical engineer turned stay-at-home mama who writes about crafty ways to encourage learning in our kids. STEAM projects are her fave.

Follow her on:

Amber Scardino
Figment Creative Labs

Amber is a mother to two active boys, a blogger and private art teacher / owner of Figment Creative Labs Art Workshops in Austin, TX.

Follow her on:

Ana Dziengel
Babble Dabble Do

Ana is an architect, award winning furniture designer, and blogger. She's now a professional crafter, amateur scientist, and art teacher to her three children.

Follow her on:

Andra Weber
Andra Weber Creative

Andra is a designer and mother who percolates creative ideas. Her blog, Create & Change Everyday, is a journey to help others find more meaning in their lives.

Follow her on:

Chelsey Marashian
Buggy and Buddy

Chelsey is a former elementary teacher, current stay-at-home mom to two kids. She strives to inspire creativity and self-confidence while promoting learning and fun.

Follow her on:

Dayna Abraham
Lemon Lime Adventures

Dayna is a National Board Certified early childhood teacher turned homeschooling mom of three. She shares ideas for intentional learning from sensory to science.

Follow her on:

Go to steamkidsbooks.com/about-us for easy links!

Erica Clark
What Do We Do All Day?

Erica is an NYC mom and a children's book and activity blogger. A self-proclaimed theater and book nerd, her two boys have nurtured in her a love of science and math.

Follow her on:

Jamie Hand
Kids STEAM Lab

Jamie is a certified art instructor and a mother of three. She writes about quick, easy and inspiring STEAM activities to grow creative kids.

Follow her on:

Karyn Tripp
Teach Beside Me

Karyn is a former educator and current homeschool parent of 4 children. She is passionate about hands-on learning and loves creating unique learning activities for families.

Follow her on:

Leslie Manlapig
Pink Stripey Socks

Leslie has degrees in engineering and psychology. She's a proud mama to two boys and loves crafting, building, and exploring with kiddos!

Follow her on:

P. R. Newton
STEAM Powered Family

Piper has a B.Sc. Psychology degree and has spent many years studying and learning about the human brain. She writes about education and childhood mental health.

Follow her on:

And come find STEAM Kids Books on Instagram, Pinterest, and Facebook for daily creative project ideas!

Check out the entire family of STEAM Kids Books for more hands-on science, technology, engineering, art, and math activity books for kids.

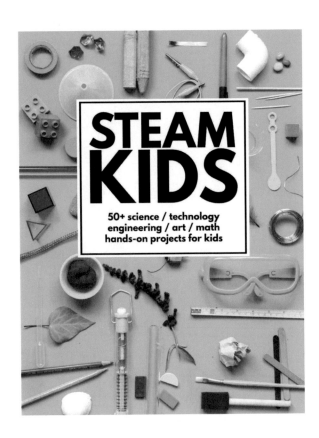

www.steamkidsbooks.com

Made in the USA
Middletown, DE
29 April 2019